Diplomatic History: A Very Short Introduction

VERY SHORT INTRODUCTIONS are for anyone wanting a stimulating and accessible way into a new subject. They are written by experts, and have been translated into more than 45 different languages.

The series began in 1995, and now covers a wide variety of topics in every discipline. The VSI library currently contains over 650 volumes—a Very Short Introduction to everything from Psychology and Philosophy of Science to American History and Relativity—and continues to grow in every subject area.

Very Short Introductions available now:

ABOLITIONISM Richard S. Newman
THE ABRAHAMIC RELIGIONS
  Charles L. Cohen
ACCOUNTING Christopher Nobes
ADOLESCENCE Peter K. Smith
ADVERTISING Winston Fletcher
AERIAL WARFARE Frank Ledwidge
AESTHETICS Bence Nanay
AFRICAN AMERICAN RELIGION
  Eddie S. Glaude Jr
AFRICAN HISTORY John Parker and
  Richard Rathbone
AFRICAN POLITICS Ian Taylor
AFRICAN RELIGIONS
  Jacob K. Olupona
AGEING Nancy A. Pachana
AGNOSTICISM Robin Le Poidevin
AGRICULTURE Paul Brassley and
  Richard Soffe
ALEXANDER THE GREAT
  Hugh Bowden
ALGEBRA Peter M. Higgins
AMERICAN BUSINESS HISTORY
  Walter A. Friedman
AMERICAN CULTURAL HISTORY
  Eric Avila
AMERICAN FOREIGN RELATIONS
  Andrew Preston
AMERICAN HISTORY
  Paul S. Boyer
AMERICAN IMMIGRATION
  David A. Gerber
AMERICAN LEGAL HISTORY
  G. Edward White

AMERICAN MILITARY HISTORY
  Joseph T. Glatthaar
AMERICAN NAVAL HISTORY
  Craig L. Symonds
AMERICAN POLITICAL HISTORY
  Donald Critchlow
AMERICAN POLITICAL PARTIES
  AND ELECTIONS L. Sandy Maisel
AMERICAN POLITICS
  Richard M. Valelly
THE AMERICAN PRESIDENCY
  Charles O. Jones
THE AMERICAN REVOLUTION
  Robert J. Allison
AMERICAN SLAVERY
  Heather Andrea Williams
THE AMERICAN SOUTH
  Charles Reagan Wilson
THE AMERICAN WEST Stephen Aron
AMERICAN WOMEN'S HISTORY
  Susan Ware
AMPHIBIANS T. S. Kemp
ANAESTHESIA Aidan O'Donnell
ANALYTIC PHILOSOPHY
  Michael Beaney
ANARCHISM Colin Ward
ANCIENT ASSYRIA Karen Radner
ANCIENT EGYPT Ian Shaw
ANCIENT EGYPTIAN ART AND
  ARCHITECTURE Christina Riggs
ANCIENT GREECE Paul Cartledge
THE ANCIENT NEAR EAST
  Amanda H. Podany
ANCIENT PHILOSOPHY Julia Annas

Available soon:

For more information visit our website

www.oup.com/vsi/

Joseph M. Siracusa

DIPLOMATIC HISTORY

A Very Short Introduction

OXFORD
UNIVERSITY PRESS

OXFORD
UNIVERSITY PRESS

Great Clarendon Street, Oxford, OX2 6DP,
United Kingdom

Oxford University Press is a department of the University of Oxford.
It furthers the University's objective of excellence in research, scholarship,
and education by publishing worldwide. Oxford is a registered trade mark of
Oxford University Press in the UK and in certain other countries

© Joseph M. Siracusa 2021

The moral rights of the author have been asserted

First edition published as Diplomacy: VSI in 2010
Second edition published as Diplomatic History: VSI in 2021

Impression: 1

Published in the United States of America by Oxford University Press
198 Madison Avenue, New York, NY 10016, United States of America

British Library Cataloguing in Publication Data
Data available

Library of Congress Control Number: 2020952675

ISBN 978-0-19-289391-8

Printed in Great Britain by
Ashford Colour Press Ltd, Gosport, Hampshire

Contents

Preface

Diplomacy has been around a very long time. British historian David Reynolds dates its origins back to at least the Bronze Age; documents from the Euphrates kingdom in the mid-8th century BC and from Akhenaten's Egypt four centuries later reveal a world of peripatetic envoys, prompted by matters of peace and war. It was primitive by today's standards; there were few rules, distances were formidable, but it was a recognizable form of diplomacy. Since then, diplomacy has evolved greatly, coming to mean different things to different people, at different times, ranging from the elegant ('an ordered conduct of relations between one group of human beings and another group alien to themselves': Harold Nicolson) to the inelegant ('the art of saying nice "doggie" until you can find a rock': Wynn Catlin). Whatever one's definition, few could doubt that the course and consequences of diplomatic history have shaped and changed the world many times over.

It is the purpose of this book to introduce the general reader to the subject and study of diplomatic history, defined broadly (though not exclusively) as the study of the management of relations between nation-states by the process of negotiations. Based on examples taken from significant historical case studies, it is designed to illustrate *diplomacy in action*, which should at once engage and instruct, while simultaneously bringing out changes in method at key historical junctures. I am not setting out to give the reader a *history of diplomacy*, which I leave to others, but rather a sense of the ways in which the practice of diplomacy varies at key historical moments. Diplomacy has its own history, of course, as institutions change, and new resources become available over time. But here, I want to use historical case studies to bring out the very different demands that circumstances make on the practice of diplomats. I also want to give some sense of the way in which skilful diplomacy, as well as hubris, rashness, and excessive caution, can have important ramifications for the fate of nations. Put another way, the case studies chosen here will demonstrate that diplomacy was and is an important element of statecraft, and that without skilful diplomacy political success may remain elusive.

Within this context, we will look briefly at the evolution of modern diplomacy, focusing on diplomats and what they do, paying particular attention to the issues they face, the strategies they employ, and the art of treaty-making, all within a historical context; the diplomacy of the American Revolution, which heralded the fateful disruption of the British Empire in the 1770s; the diplomatic origins of the Great War and its aftermath Versailles, which carried away five empires (the Austro-Hungarian, German, Italian, Japanese, and the Ottoman) and an entire generation of young men; the personal summitry behind the night Stalin and Churchill divided Europe, which foreshadowed the coming of the Cold War; George W. Bush and the Iraq War, which marked the triumph of the militarization of American diplomacy and an era of endless wars; and, finally, diplomacy in the age of globalization, which opened up new pathways for the conduct of diplomacy while facilitating the involvement of new participants, against the backdrop of America's global retreat and the recrudescence of Great Power Competition.

After factoring out the obvious differences such as the various systems of government that each age of diplomacy represented and the communications revolution that was profoundly important, especially for modern summitry, what each of these case studies has in common is *the universal role of negotiations*. In the chapters that follow, the diplomat *qua* negotiator always attempts to achieve an agreement which is somewhat better than the realities of his fundamental position would justify, and which is, in any case, not worse than his fundamental position requires. This is as true in relations between nation-states as in relations between organizations and individuals. Not all succeeded, of course—some more than others. Meanwhile, each had to make sure of his constituency while making equally sure that his opposite number had control of his. Among the cases under consideration, high marks go to the colonial diplomats of the American Revolution whose realism compelled them to think and act in terms of power, eschewing ideology and moral principles. There was, in fact, precious little room to manoeuvre, and the fear of failure was a constant companion. Benjamin Franklin's timely warning that the colonies either could hang together or one at a time ultimately translated itself into the brilliant outcome achieved by the revolutionary diplomats who seldom failed to take advantage of Europe's distresses. And this was all done at a time when it could take a month or more for a letter to travel from Philadelphia to Paris!

And, like the other diplomatic episodes found in this volume, the historical repercussions could be profound. The disruption of the British Empire in the 1770s, for example, was one of the fateful events of modern history. Had British statesmanship then been capable of the levels of wisdom it attained in the next century, a British–American or American–British Commonwealth of Nations might have guided the world along paths of peaceful development with little to fear from Imperial Germany, Nazi Germany, or Communist Russia. Such a might-have-been is the stuff of virtual history and an endless, fascinating subject of counterfactuals. Similarly, the best statecraft of Bismarck's classic diplomacy in the run-up to the 20th century could do nothing to avoid the drift towards the abyss of war. Consequently, as historian

Arnold Toynbee so aptly writes, Western civilization was about to enter a 'time of troubles', comparable to the self-destructive rage that afflicted the city-states of ancient Greece. Or, to quote Henry Kissinger, wearing his diplomatic historian's hat: 'Since nothing about the First World War had gone as planned, it was inevitable that the quest for peace would prove as futile as the expectations with which nations had launched themselves into the catastrophe.' For all their efforts, the diplomats at Versailles achieved the precise opposite of what they had set out to do, inexorably, tragically laying the groundwork for the next, more horrible world war. In this sense, then, the story of diplomacy also reads as a cautionary tale, in the long history of unintended consequences.

Apropos acknowledgements, I should like to express my gratitude to Latha Menon for suggesting the topic Diplomatic History, which pivots away from my original approach but not the subject matter in *Diplomacy: A Very Short Introduction* (2010), upon which *Diplomatic History* rests. I should also like to thank Jenny Nugee for her enthusiasm and professionalism in making it happen. Also, I should be remiss if I did not thank the anonymous Delegates for their thoughtful reviews and constructive criticism; even those who do not always agree with me gave me much food for thought. My intellectual debts are at once overwhelming and plain to see, as recognized in the text and References and further reading. Needless to say—but I will say it anyway—I am alone responsible for the text that follows.

Professor Joseph M. Siracusa
Melbourne

List of illustrations

Chapter 1
Evolution of diplomacy

Traditional diplomacy has been most importantly concerned with the transition from a state of peace to a state of war, and vice versa; in other words, dealing with the interface of conflict and peace-making. And while this is a central aspect of diplomatic activities in the past and present, it should also be noted that it is today only one, important, aspect. Diplomacy has become something very much more than the diplomacy of states and governments. Though it is still true that the legal formalities based on the 1961 Vienna Convention on Diplomatic Relations acknowledge only the diplomacy of states, on the ground, it is impossible to ignore the diplomacy of the global economic system, from the activities of TNCs (transnational corporations) to the intervention of the global economic IGOs (intergovernmental organizations), particularly the World Trade Organization. These, in turn, have diplomatic webs which operate both within and outside the traditional diplomatic system. The same is true of another vast area of diplomatic activity, the diplomacy of civil society organizations. Moreover, the saga of failed and failing states, international terrorism, and the COVID-19 pandemic has created a radically new global world of urgent communications between states and NGOs (non-governmental organizations), between NGOs and IGOs, and amongst NGOs themselves. These developments will be dealt within Chapter 6.

The evolution of diplomacy

The roots of the word 'diplomacy' can be traced back to the ancient Greeks—the normal word for a diplomat in Classical Greece was, in fact, the word for an old man—and was later used by the French (*diplomatie*) to refer to the work of a negotiator. There is, of course, a long history of diplomatic activity going back literally thousands of years. The earliest diplomatic record extant is a letter inscribed on a tablet which has been dated around 2500 BC, found in present-day northern Iran; it apparently was carried by an emissary who had made a round trip of nearly 1,200 miles between distant kingdoms. Sovereigns traditionally sent envoys to other sovereigns for various reasons: to prevent wars, cease hostilities, conclude treaties, or merely continue peaceful relations and further trade. The modern era of diplomacy is conventionally dated to the Peace of Westphalia in 1648, which ended hostilities in the Thirty Years War. It also established the independence of states and the notion of religious freedom and toleration. The first foreign ministry was created in 1626 by France's Cardinal Richelieu (Figure 1), who also introduced the classic approach to international relations, based on the nation-state and motivated by national interest as its goal. In the 18th century, Great Britain placed its diplomacy in the service of the balance of power, while in the 19th century, Metternich's Austria used its diplomacy to reconstruct the so-called Concert of Europe—a consensus among the Great Powers to maintain the European balance of power and the integrity of territorial boundaries—only to have it dismantled by Bismarck's Germany, reshaping European diplomacy, in Henry Kissinger's words, 'into a cold-blooded game of power politics'.

As divine-right kings gave way to constitutional monarchies and republics, embassies and legations became more and more institutionalized all over Europe, and by the beginning of the 20th century, European-style diplomacy had ultimately been

1. **Cardinal Richelieu.**

adopted throughout the entire international community. It was a
fully-fledged diplomatic system. Large countries had embassies
in other large countries and legations in smaller countries.
Embassies were headed by ambassadors and legations by

ministers. Whether a diplomatic mission was given the rank of an embassy or legation—whether its chief was an ambassador or minister—formerly depended upon the importance that the two governments attached to their mutual relations. During the first century of its existence, for example, the United States maintained only legations abroad, and, reciprocally, foreign governments kept only legations in the American capital. In 1893, Congress provided for the elevation of several of the more important legations to embassies, on a reciprocal basis. Thereafter, embassies gradually replaced legations until 1966, when the last American legations (Bulgaria and Hungary) became embassies. The change was indicative of the growing importance that the United States attached to its diplomacy.

Public diplomacy

Embassies and legations were once strictly limited in their contacts with the ordinary citizens of the host state. These limitations were eventually codified in the Havana Convention of 1928, which under the heading 'Duties of Diplomatic Officers' required that these officers were not to interfere in the internal affairs of the host state and must confine their relations to official communications. Thus, diplomatic personnel from abroad had no formal relations with the public at large in the receiving state. Prior to the Second World War, then, diplomacy was essentially a government-to-government relationship, in the sense that Foreign Diplomatic Officers were discouraged from participating in the domestic or foreign policies of the state in which they exercised their function. However, the Convention manifestly did not go so far as to say diplomats should have no contact with foreign citizens. This would have been unrealistic, since reporting on conditions in states of their accreditation has been a recognized function of resident missions since their invention in the 15th century, and they could have hardly done this without meeting with private citizens, albeit usually those confined to the local political, commercial, and financial elites. The stipulation restricting 'official communications' to foreign ministries was designed chiefly to protect the position of such ministries relative to other ministries—not relative to the citizenry in general—and thereby avoid chaos in bilateral relations.

Since the end of the Second World War, and for a number of reasons, especially the pressures of the Cold War and the international war on terror, the practice of diplomacy has been broadened to include a distinctive government-to-people connection, broadly known as public diplomacy. It basically refers to the influence of public attitudes on the formation and execution of foreign policies. Coined in 1965 by Edmund Gullion, a US career diplomat, public diplomacy literally reaches beyond traditional diplomacy, aiming at the cultivation by governments of public opinion in other countries. Equally important, it openly sponsors the interaction of private groups and interests in one country with those of another, facilitated by the transnational flow of information and ideas.

Public diplomacy, according to Charles Wolf and Brian Rosen, can best be understood by contrasting its principal characteristics with those of *official* diplomacy. First, public diplomacy is transparent and widely disseminated, whereas official diplomacy is not; second, public diplomacy is transmitted by governments to wider, or in some cases selected, publics (especially those in the Middle East or the Muslim world), whereas official diplomacy is transmitted by governments to other governments; and, third, the themes and issues with which official diplomacy is concerned relate to the behaviour and policies of governments, whereas the themes and issues with which public diplomacy is concerned relate to the attitudes and behaviours of publics. Always open to charges of propaganda and interference in the internal affairs of other nations, public diplomacy clearly challenged both the spirit and letter of the Havana Convention.

Diplomats and treaties

Traditional diplomacy has also been greatly concerned with making treaties. The *Oxford English Dictionary* defines 'treaty' variously: in a narrow sense, as a 'contract between two or more states, relating to peace, truce alliance, commerce or other international relations', and, more broadly, as 'a settlement or arrangement arrived at by treaty or negotiating, in the sense of an agreement, covenant, or contract'. It could have also said something about the distinction between the specific meanings of 'convention' and 'treaty', but it didn't. Whereas in the 19th century, the term 'convention' was regularly employed for bilateral agreements, in the 20th century it was generally employed for formal multilateral treaties, with a broad number of parties. Usually the instruments negotiated under the auspices of an international organization such as the United Nations are entitled 'conventions'. In bilateral relations, the term is often applied to treaties of a technical or social character such as those on social security or double taxation.

Whichever name is used, the power to enter into treaty relations—the most formal and highest instrument of agreement between nations, almost always undertaken by diplomatic practitioners—is an essential attribute of sovereignty. The principle that treaties validly concluded are binding on the signatories, who must adhere to them in good faith, is a cardinal rule in international law. It is also the very basis of the modern system of international relations. The usual conditions essential to the valid conclusion of a treaty are that the contracting parties have the requisite capacity to enter into international engagements, the plenipotentiaries who negotiate them must be properly recognized, and there is freedom of action on the part of the signatory powers. It is also recognized that a treaty is void if its conclusions have been procured by the threat or use of force in violation of the principles of international law embodied in the United Nations Charter. Peace treaties concluded after cessation of hostilities were usually considered to be valid because of preceding warfare. Nevertheless, the United States established a policy not to recognize any treaty or agreement brought about by means contrary to the Kellogg–Briand Pact (1928)—or Peace of Paris—by which the USA joined the other nations of the world in renouncing war as an instrument of national policy. The principle is known as the Stimson Doctrine, named after the Secretary of State Henry Stimson, who in 1931 formally expressed American opposition to the Japanese conquest of Manchuria, while refusing to accept any changes in territorial possession as a consequence of the invasion. The Stimson Doctrine was adopted by the League of Nations. Similar principles were included in the 1969 Vienna Convention on the Law of Treaties.

On the international level, the scope of the treaty-making power of a state is practically unlimited. It includes the acquisition of foreign territory, the cession of domestic territory, the delimitation and rectification of boundaries, the promise of mutual assistance, the guarantee of foreign investments, and the extradition of persons accused or convicted of crimes. Treaties may be of a law-making character and of a multinational nature, such as the conventions on the law of the sea and on the privileges and immunities of diplomatic missions and their staff. Multilateral treaties are also the basis for the establishment of international organizations and the determination of their individual functions and powers.

Many treaties can be classified as either political or commercial arrangements. Political treaties especially may relate to mutual defence in case of an armed attack; to guarantees of a particular state, such as neutrality; or to the preservation of existing boundaries. The concept of collective security—the idea of a universal, permanent, and collective commitment to oppose aggression while guaranteeing security—was an important innovation of 20th-century international relations. It was embedded in the Covenant of the League of Nations (Article X), at the insistence of Woodrow Wilson, and re-emerged in a modified form in the United Nations Charter. Commercial treaties usually provide mutual economic advantage, such as reduced tariffs on the imported products of the parties to the agreement. In modern times, such treaties often contain a clause stipulating that each signatory will extend to every other signatory treatment equally favourable to that accorded to any other nation (the 'most-favoured-nation' clause). The most important multilateral treaty of that type is the General Agreement on Tariffs and Trade (GATT). Another class of treaties provides for the submission of disputes to arbitration by special tribunals or to adjudication by institutions such as the Permanent Court of Arbitration or International Court of Justice.

International law prescribes neither a fixed form for a treaty nor any fixed procedure for its conclusion. It may be concluded by an exchange of diplomatic notes incorporating an agreed-upon text signed by authorized officials, or by the signing of one or more copies of the text by officials authorized to express the consent of their respective governments to be bound by the treaty. Many important treaties require ratification by each of the contracting parties. In such cases, the negotiators, after reaching agreement on the final text, sign the document and then submit the proposed treaty for ratification to the constitutionally authorized authority, usually the head of state or head of the government. In some countries—and at certain times—the procedures have been easy and predictable. When the supreme leader of the Soviet Union, Joseph Stalin, wanted a non-aggression pact with Adolf Hitler in August 1939 (the Nazi–Soviet Pact), there were no bars or procedures. In other cases, the treaty process becomes quite complex and politically charged, and the outcome uncertain.

Treaties are considered binding (*pacta sunt servanda*) but may be terminated in various ways. The treaty itself may provide for its termination at a specified time, or it may allow one party to give notice of termination, effective either at the time of receipt or following the expiration of a specified period. A treaty may be terminated by one signatory's repudiation of its obligation; such a unilateral termination, however, may provoke retaliatory measures. A treaty may lapse naturally, through war or renunciation, or at other times by reliance on the principle *rebus sic stantibus* (things remaining that way), that is, when the state of affairs assumed by the signatory parties (when they signed the treaty, and therefore the real basis of the treaty) no longer exists and a substantial change in conditions has taken place. Notably, the doctrine of changed circumstances leading to termination is not generally applied to fundamental treaties of communal application such as the United Nations Charter or the Geneva Conventions. Examples of both abound in diplomatic history: Imperial Japan and Nazi Germany both gave formal notice to quit the League of Nations, while the great Cold War alliance arrangements such as SEATO and the Warsaw Pact fell away. More recently, the United States served notice that it was quitting the ABM (Anti-Ballistic Missile) Treaty with the former Soviet Union, the Russian Federation.

The Vienna Convention on the Law of Treaties

Rules of international law governing the conclusion, validity, effects, interpretation, modification, suspension, and termination of treaties were codified in the Vienna Convention on the Law of Treaties, adopted in 1969, at a conference convened by a resolution of the United Nations General Assembly. Representatives from 110 nations participated, including those from the United States, Great Britain, France, the Soviet Union, and most other United Nations members, as well as several non-members, including Switzerland. The draft was prepared by the International Law Commission. The Convention went into force in January 1980 after ratification by thirty-five nations. The United States signed but has not yet ratified the Convention; however, the United States considers most of the Vienna Convention's rules as representing customary international law.

Treaties of international peace and cooperation comprise nothing less than the diplomatic landscape of human history: from the benchmark European treaties of the Congress of Vienna (1815), Brest-Litovsk (1918), and Versailles (1919) to the milestone events such as the Covenant of the League of Nations (1919), the United Nations Charter (1948), and the North Atlantic Treaty Organization (1949). Treaties impacting on international peace and disarmament have had surprising durability. The conclusion of the Limited Test Ban Treaty between the United States, the United Kingdom, and the Soviet Union, in 1963, which banned signatories from conducting atmospheric and above-ground nuclear explosions, marked the turning point in the Cold War. The superpowers moved a step closer to nuclear sanity. The 1968 Treaty on the Non-Proliferation of Nuclear Weapons, or NPT, with its 190 signatories, remains the sole global, legal, and diplomatic barrier to the spread of nuclear weapons. The NPT successfully created an international standard against the spread of nuclear weapons, while establishing an international inspection regime that remains the last best hope to prevent the diversion of nuclear reactor fuel to weapons of mass destruction. Diplomacy and diplomats are today the keys to resolving the greatest challenges of the 21st century, including nuclear proliferation (Iran and North Korea, for openers), global warming, and the aftermath of the COVID-19 pandemic, often touching outside the zero-sum game of inter-state competition.

Within this context, then, the historical case studies that follow deal with the course and consequences of the major events of modern international diplomacy, paying particular attention to how the art of diplomacy—the principal moderating institution of international politics—has changed and shaped the world in which we live. This story begins in the last quarter of the 18th century, as British colonials in the New World, first, take on the might of the British Empire, then, negotiate their freedom.

Chapter 2
Diplomacy of the American Revolution

With the conclusion of the Seven Years War in 1763, Great Britain commanded the greatest empire since the fall of Rome. Victory, however, brought with it the necessity of reorganizing the vast North American territories wrested from France and Spain. To prevent further warfare with Native Americans, the Proclamation of 1763 closed the vast trans-Appalachian area to white settlement. With a view to defending and policing these new territories, the British government maintained an unprecedented standing army in mainland America. To meet the costs of this commitment, as well as to relieve the massive financial burden left by the war, London sought to impose new taxes and enforce imperial trade laws that had long been ignored by the colonists. The end of the French and Indian War—as the Seven Years War was known in America—thus marked the end of the period of so-called 'salutary neglect'.

British measures were designed not only to bring peace and stability to North America, but also to require the colonies to share the cost of imperial defence and administration. The colonies, however, had come to think of themselves as self-governing entities, as having 'dominion status', to use a term of later origin, and they refused to have their duties prescribed for them by parliament and king. Parliament and King George III were unwilling to accept such a novel theory of empire. Great Britain, consequently, found itself involved in a war, not only with its colonies, but eventually with most of Europe. The war, though not wholly disastrous to British arms, deprived Great Britain of the most valuable of its colonial possessions and cast it down from the pinnacle of power that the country had attained by the Peace of Paris of 1763.

The initial aim of armed revolt was not independence, but rather a restoration and recognition of what the colonials held to be their rights as British subjects. They professed to have been content with their status under British policy prior to 1763. That the colonies turned to independence in the second year of the struggle was partly the consequence of the British government's rejection of compromise and its adoption, instead, of severe repressive measures. It was also the consequence of a dawning realization of the advantages that might accrue from independence. No one set forth the arguments for independence so persuasively as a recent immigrant from England named Thomas Paine. Paine had arrived in America in late 1774, leaving behind a number of failed careers. Less than two years later, in January 1776, he published the pamphlet *Common Sense*. This pamphlet sold some 120,000 copies in the first three months and was the single most effective articulation of the case for independence. Among Paine's arguments, two were significant for the future foreign policy of the United States. Independence, argued Paine, would free the former colonies from being entangled in European wars in which they had no concern. A declaration of independence would also improve their chances of securing foreign aid.

The quest for foreign aid

Greatly inferior to the mother country in numbers, wealth, industry, and military and naval power, the colonies could hardly hope for decisive military success unless aided by one of the major European powers. Months before deciding upon independence, Congress had set up a secret committee to contact friends abroad.

This committee had sent to Paris a secret agent in the guise of a merchant to seek supplies and credit. The agent, Silas Deane of Connecticut, arriving in Paris in July 1776, soon found that the French government was disposed to give secret assistance to Britain's rebelling colonies. French ministers, in fact, had been on the lookout since 1763 for an opportunity to weaken and humiliate France's victorious rival, Great Britain. The celebrated French playwright and amateur diplomat Caron de Beaumarchais, who had already been in contact with another colonial agent, Arthur Lee, in London, believed that such an opportunity had now arrived. So too believed the Comte de Vergennes, French Foreign Minister, and Vergennes and Beaumarchais were able to persuade King Louis XVI that aid to the colonies was in the French interest.

As yet, however, France was not willing to openly avow its friendship for the colonies and offered material aid only in secret. This was managed through the creation by Beaumarchais of a fictitious commercial firm, Rodrigue Hortalez et Compagnie, through which gunpowder and other essential supplies from the French arsenals were channelled to the armies of George Washington. Spain, too, was persuaded by France to give aid through this and other means. All in all, measured in the dollars of that day, France contributed to the American cause nearly $2,000,000 in subsidies and over $6,350,000 in loans; Spain, approximately $400,000 and $250,000 in subsidies and loans, respectively.

The French alliance

These arrangements for secret 'lend-lease' had been instituted before Deane's arrival in Paris. After the Declaration of Independence, Congress sent to France the most widely known, most admired, and most persuasive American of his day, Benjamin Franklin (Figure 2). In Paris, he joined Deane and Arthur Lee, who had come from London, to form a three-man American commission. The commission's work was severely

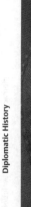

2. Benjamin Franklin.

compromised by enemy agents, leading the historian Jonathon Dull to label it 'virtually an unemployment bureau for the British secret service'. The most important of British agents was Dr Edward Bancroft, a native of Massachusetts who had been employed as Deane's secretary. Bancroft was secretly in the pay of the British government, to which he faithfully reported the work of the commission and its relations with the French ministers. Arthur Lee was convinced of Bancroft's treachery but could not shake Franklin's and Deane's faith in their employee. In addition to the presence of enemy agents, Franklin frequently leaked information for political reasons, while Deane used inside information in pursuit of speculative schemes.

The principal purpose of Franklin's mission was to secure from the French government official recognition of the United States as an independent nation. Recognition could be accomplished by the signing of a treaty between France and the United States. Franklin brought with him to Paris a draft of a proposed Treaty of Amity and Commerce, which had been prepared by a committee of Congress and which embodied the liberal commercial principles that Congress hoped to see adopted, not only by France but by the entire trading world. This Plan of Treaties of 1776 was the first major state paper dealing with American foreign policy and would guide the makers of such policy far beyond the exigencies of the Revolution. John Adams, the principal author of the model treaty, repeatedly asserted that any Franco-American treaty should take the form of a commercial connection with no military or political ties. Adams said of France:

> We ought not to enter into any Alliance with her, which should entangle Us in any future Wars in Europe, ... We ought to lay it down as a first principle and a Maxim never to be forgotten, to maintain an entire Neutrality in all future European Wars.

Though friendly to the United States, Vergennes was unwilling to grant formal recognition, thus risking war with Britain, until the Americans could offer some evidence of their ability to do their share in winning the war. Quite understandably, he did not wish to involve France in a war for a losing cause. Such evidence was not forthcoming until December 1777, when news arrived that General Burgoyne's British army, thrusting down from Montreal into New York, had been forced to surrender to General Gates at Saratoga. This was what Vergennes had been waiting for; he tried to enlist Spain in the cause, and when Spain procrastinated, resolved that France should proceed without it.

On 17 December, the American commissioners were informed that France would grant recognition and make a treaty with the United States. On 6 February 1778, a Treaty of Amity and Commerce and a Treaty of Alliance were signed in Paris, the latter to take effect if Great Britain went to war with France because of the former. The Treaty of Amity and Commerce clearly reflected the principles set down by Adams in the Plan of Treaties of 1776. The Treaty of Alliance, however, ran contrary to his calls to avoid an alliance with France 'which might embarrass Us in after times and involve Us in future European Wars'.

Vergennes had hastened to take this action out of fear that Great Britain would effect a reconciliation with its former colonies. Burgoyne's surrender had produced a sensation in Britain and led the ministry to offer liberal terms of settlement to the Americans. In March, Parliament passed a series of bills repealing all the legislation enacted since 1763 of which the colonists had complained. In April, a commission headed by the Earl of Carlisle was dispatched to America, empowered to offer Congress virtually everything it had claimed, independence alone excepted, if the former colonies would lay down their arms and resume their allegiance to the British Crown. The right to control their own taxation, to elect their governors and other officials formerly appointed, to be represented in Parliament if they so desired, to continue Congress as an American legislature, release from quitrents (rent paid in lieu of required feudal services), assurance that their colonial charters would not be altered without their consent, and full pardon for all who had engaged in rebellion—these terms of the offer indicate how far Great Britain was willing to go to save its empire from disruption. In effect, it was offering 'dominion status' to America.

Had such an offer been made at any time prior to the Declaration of Independence, perhaps at any time prior to Burgoyne's surrender, it might well have been accepted, and the troublesome thirteen states would have become the first British dominion. The offer came too late. With recognition and the promise of an alliance and open aid from France, independence seemed assured, and there was no turning back. Congress ratified the treaties with France without even stopping to parley with the Carlisle Commission.

The Treaty of Amity and Commerce placed each nation on a most-favoured-nation basis with reference to the other and embodied, practically unaltered, the liberal principles of the 'Plan of 1776'—principles which would protect the interest of either signatory that might chance to be neutral when the other was at war. The Treaty of Alliance was to go into effect if France should become embroiled in the existing war against Great Britain. Its object was 'to maintain effectually the liberty, Sovereignty, and independence absolute and unlimited' of the United States. France renounced forever any designs upon Bermuda or upon any parts of the continent of North America which before the Treaty of Paris of 1763 or by virtue of that treaty had belonged to Great Britain or the former British colonies. It reserved the right to possess itself of any of the British West Indian colonies. The United States, on the other hand, was free to conquer and hold Bermuda or any of Great Britain's mainland possessions. Neither party was to make a separate peace with Great Britain nor lay down its arms until American independence was won. Both parties mutually guaranteed 'from the present time and forever against all other powers' the American possessions which they then held and with which they might emerge from the war. France, in addition, undertook to guarantee the liberty, sovereignty, and independence of the United States.

The treaty just described constituted the only 'entangling alliance' in which the United States participated until the middle of the

20th century. And it was to cause serious embarrassment before it was set aside in 1800, but in the winning of independence, it was indispensable. A French army under General Rochambeau was sent to America, and French fleets under Admirals d'Estaing and de Grasse operated off the American coast. The importance of French aid is illustrated by the fact that in the final scene of the Revolution, at Yorktown, Cornwallis's British army was caught between a French fleet and an allied army, of which two-thirds were French.

Spain and the Revolution

Spain, though bound to France by a dynastic alliance, the 'Family Compact', and though giving secret aid to the United States, hung back from entering the war for over a year after France became a belligerent. There were advantages that Spain might gain from a successful war with Great Britain, namely the recovery of Gibraltar (lost in 1713) and of Florida (lost in 1763). Gibraltar, the more valuable of these, the Spanish court hoped to regain peaceably, as a reward for mediating between Great Britain and France. Only when Great Britain declined the proffered service did Spain sign a definite alliance with France—the Convention of Aranjuez, 12 April 1779—and declare war against Great Britain, on 21 June 1779. The Franco-American Treaty of Alliance had reserved for Spain the right to become a member, but Spain declined to sign it or to make any kind of treaty with the United States. A colonial power itself, Spain naturally hesitated to give formal acknowledgement to a rebellion of the colonies of Great Britain. John Jay spent many bitter months in Madrid asking in vain for recognition. Even an offer to waive the American claim of right to navigate the Mississippi River could not persuade the Spanish government to recognize the young republic. By the Convention of Aranjuez, France and Spain agreed that neither would make peace until Spain had recovered Gibraltar. Since the United States had promised not to make peace without France, it could not, if all treaty engagements were observed, make peace until Gibraltar was restored to Spain.

In America, Spanish interests ran counter to those of the United States. The United States desired the Mississippi River as its western boundary and the right of navigating the river through Spanish territory to the Gulf of Mexico. Spain, anxious to monopolize as far as possible the navigation and commerce of both river and gulf, was unwilling to concede to the Americans either the use of the river or a foothold on its eastern bank. If the Spanish had their way, the western boundary of the United States would be fixed as near as possible to the summit of the Appalachians.

The bargaining position of Spain was strengthened by the daring and vigour of Bernardo de Galvez, the young governor of Louisiana. Less than two years after Spain's entry into the war, he had routed the British out of West Florida, from Natchez in the north, to Pensacola in the east. He established Spain's claim to a cession of Florida at the end of the war and to full control of the lower Mississippi.

A pawn in the European chess game

In order to win independence, the United States had found it necessary to involve itself in the international rivalries and politics of Europe. Those same rivalries and politics, however, threatened to terminate the war with American independence still unwon. Spain, having entered the war reluctantly, soon grew tired of it. In 1780, the Spanish government received a British mission, come to discuss peace terms. For America, the Spanish ministers proposed a long truce between Great Britain and its 'colonies', without specific recognition of independence and with a division of territory on the basis of *uti possidetis*, or retention by each party of the areas then occupied. This would have left the British in control of Maine, the northern frontier, New York City, Long Island, and the principal seaports south of Virginia.

Vergennes disapproved of these Anglo-Spanish conversations, which violated the Convention of Aranjuez. He was willing to listen, however, to proposals for mediation from the Tsarina Catherine II of Russia and the Austrian Emperor, Joseph II, which would have had much the same effect in America. John Adams, who had been named American peace commissioner and came from The Hague to Paris at Vergennes's behest, rejected the proposal out of hand when Vergennes laid it before him. No truce, he said, until all British troops were withdrawn from the United States; no negotiation with Great Britain without guarantees that American sovereignty and independence would be respected. But in America, Congress was more easily persuaded than was Adams. Under pressure (and in some instances monetary persuasion) from Anne-César de La Luzerne, the French minister, Congress, on 15 June 1781, drew up new instructions to its prospective peace commissioners in Europe. Not only were they directed to accept the mediation of the Tsarina and the Emperor; they were to place themselves in the hands of the French ministers, 'to undertake nothing in the negotiations for peace or truce without their knowledge and concurrence', and ultimately to be governed 'by their advice and opinion'. It was perhaps fortunate for the United States that the British government rejected the proposal for mediation.

Great Britain in difficulty

The surrender of Cornwallis to Washington and Rochambeau at Yorktown, 19 October 1781, was the climax of Great Britain's misfortunes. The country was now at war, or on the verge of war, with most of the Western world. To the list of its open enemies, Great Britain had itself added the Netherlands, forcing the Dutch into war rather than permit continuance of their neutral trade with France. The Baltic countries, Russia, Denmark, and Sweden, had in 1780 organized themselves into a League of Armed Neutrality for the purpose of protecting their commerce against what they considered the illegitimate exactions of the British navy; and they had been joined by Prussia, the Emperor (of the Holy Roman Empire), the Kingdom of the Two Sicilies, and even Portugal, Great Britain's traditional ally. There was little that the British could hope to gain by prolonging the war.

In February 1782, following receipt of the news of the disaster at Yorktown, the British House of Commons resolved that the war ought to be terminated. In March, the ministry of Lord North, whose policies had precipitated the American conflict, resigned, and a new ministry headed by the Marquis of Rockingham took office. The Earl of Shelburne, as Secretary of State for the Southern Department, initiated peace talks by sending Richard Oswald, a Scot, to confer with the American representatives in Paris. After Rockingham's death in July 1782, Shelburne became Prime Minister but continued to guide negotiations with the United States. This was fortunate, for Shelburne was an advocate of a generous peace, which might result in recapturing for Great Britain the bulk of American trade and, at some future date, perhaps, tempt the United States back into some sort of imperial federation.

The American Congress named five peace commissioners, of whom three actually handled the negotiations. Franklin was in Paris when the talks began. John Jay, who had been vainly seeking recognition and a treaty in Madrid, arrived in June 1782. John Adams, who had secured recognition and a loan from the Netherlands, reached Paris in October. Henry Laurens was on hand in time to sign the treaty. Thomas Jefferson, the fifth of those named by Congress, declined to serve. Most of the work was done by Franklin and Jay, with Adams giving valuable aid towards the close of the negotiations.

The stakes of diplomacy

The American commissioners had three principal objectives:
(1) recognition of independence, which was now assured; (2) the
widest boundaries obtainable; (3) retention of the inshore
fishing privileges on the coasts of British North America that the
colonials had enjoyed as British subjects. The British government
was ready to recognize American independence and to act
generously on the other American demands. It hoped in turn to
secure from the United States: (1) provision for the payment of
the pre-revolutionary debts of American planters and others to
British creditors; and (2) an agreement to compensate the
Loyalists (Americans who had sided with Great Britain in the
struggle) for the lands and other property that had been seized by
the states in which they lived.

Of the American demands, the most controversial was that
concerning boundaries, for American claims on this point
involved not only adjustments with Great Britain, but also
disputes with Spain—disputes in which Vergennes chose to
support his Spanish rather than his American ally. In their more
sanguine moments, Benjamin Franklin and other American
leaders dreamed of including in their confederacy the whole of
British North America and certain outlying islands. Such hopes
had no chance of fulfilment. What the United States Congress laid
claim to as a matter of right was the entire western country
between the Appalachian Mountains and the Mississippi River,
extending from the 31st parallel on the south to a northern line
drawn from the St Lawrence River at north latitude 45° to Lake
Nipissing (the south-western boundary of Quebec before 1774)
and thence to the source of the Mississippi. These claims, based
chiefly upon the sea-to-sea clauses in certain colonial charters,
had never been taken seriously by the British government, which
in the years since 1763 had acted upon the theory that the western
lands still belonged to the Crown.

South of the Ohio River, American settlements in central Kentucky and eastern and central Tennessee gave the United States a solid basis for claiming those areas, but farther south it was the Spanish, not the Americans, who had driven the British out. The Spanish held the east bank of the Mississippi as far north as Natchez. They hoped, as was previously noted, to deny the Americans access to the Mississippi and to draw the boundary as near as possible to the Appalachian watershed. In this endeavour they had French support.

In the summer of 1779, Congress had taken the first step towards peace negotiations by naming John Adams commissioner for that purpose. In instructions prepared for him on 14 August 1779, it proposed boundaries including the entire area claimed by the states from the mountains to the Mississippi. It added that although it was 'of the utmost importance to the peace and Commerce of the United States that Canada and Nova Scotia should be ceded', and that equal rights in the fisheries should be guaranteed, a desire to terminate the war had led Congress to refrain from making the acquisition of these objects an ultimatum. Subsequently, under stress of military necessity and pressure from the French minister, Congress modified those demands. In the new instructions of 15 June 1781, it insisted only upon independence and the preservation of the treaties with France as indispensable conditions. With regard to boundaries, the commissioners were to regard the earlier instructions as indicating 'the desires and expectations of Congress' but were not to adhere to them if they presented an obstacle to peace. The task of the commissioners was to get as much as they could of the terms proposed two years earlier. In this respect, they were quite successful.

The peace negotiations

The first obstacles encountered by the Americans were erected by the Spanish and French, not by the British. When John Jay arrived in Paris, suspicious of both Spain and France after his futile mission in Madrid, he found disturbing confirmation of his distrust. Conversations with the Spanish ambassador in Paris and with a spokesman for Vergennes showed that the Spanish, with French support, were bent upon excluding the United States from the Mississippi Valley. French support of Spanish claims impaired the confidential relations between Vergennes and the American commissioners. Vergennes had previously agreed that the American and French negotiations should proceed separately but at equal pace and with the understanding that neither settlement should become effective without the other. Franklin and Jay now proceeded to negotiate their own preliminary terms with the British, neglecting, with considerable justification, to make those 'most candid and confidential communications' to the French ministers enjoined upon them by their instructions of 15 June 1781. In negotiating their settlement with Great Britain, they simply disregarded Spanish claims in the western country north of the 31st parallel, assuming (as did the British) that that country was still Great Britain's to dispose of.

In informal talks with Oswald, Franklin had already sketched what, as an American, he considered the 'necessary' and the 'advisable' terms of a lasting peace. Among 'necessary' terms he included, after independence and withdrawal of troops, 'a confinement of the boundaries of Canada' to what they had been before the Quebec Act (that is, the St Lawrence–Nipissing line), 'if not to a still more contracted state', and the retention of fishing privileges. Among 'advisable' terms which might be expected to contribute to a permanent reconciliation, he mentioned indemnification by Great Britain of those persons who had been ruined through the devastations of war, acknowledgement of error expressed in an Act of Parliament or in some other public document, admission of American ships and trade to British and Irish ports upon the same terms as those of Britain, and 'giving up every part of Canada'.

A delay in the negotiations now ensued, first because Oswald had no formal commission as an agent of the British government, and after his commission arrived on 8 August, because it failed to authorize him to recognize the independence of the United States as preliminary to negotiation but, on the contrary, empowered him to treat with representatives of 'colonies' of Great Britain. It did, however, authorize him to make recognition of independence the first article of the proposed treaty. Franklin and Jay were at first inclined to insist upon formal recognition of independence as a condition precedent to negotiation; but, becoming alarmed lest France use any further delay to their disadvantage, they agreed to accept as recognition a new commission that authorized Oswald to treat with commissioners of the United States of America. In this meticulous stickling for matters of form, and with the passage of time, the situation was modified to the disadvantage of the United States.

On 1 September, instructions were sent to Oswald to agree to terms of peace on the basis of the 'necessary' terms proposed by Franklin, conceding to the United States the western country as far north as the Nipissing line, and making no stipulation for the payment of pre-war debts or the restitution of property confiscated from the Loyalists. A draft of a treaty on these terms was initialled by the commissioners on 5 October and referred to London. The unfortunate results of delay now became apparent. News had arrived in London of the failure of a major assault upon Gibraltar, which had been besieged for three years by Spanish and French land and sea forces. With this victory in hand, Shelburne took a firmer tone towards the United States. He not only insisted that something be done for creditors and Loyalists, but made a last-minute attempt to hold the north-west, though this latter move may have been merely a gesture designed to secure concessions on the other points. 'They wanted', Franklin reported, 'to bring their boundary down to the Ohio and to settle the loyalists in the Illinois country. We did not choose such neighbors.'

The Americans, now reinforced by Adams, insisted upon retention of the north-west, but were ready to make concessions on this and other points. They agreed to inclusion in the treaty of articles in the interest of the Loyalists and the British creditors. They accepted the St Croix River instead of the St John, which Congress had originally proposed, as the north-eastern boundary, thereby laying the basis of a controversy which took sixty years to settle. In the west, they dropped the Nipissing line proposal, agreeing to accept instead either of two alternatives: a line drawn due west along the 45th parallel from the St Lawrence to the Mississippi, or a line through the middle of the St Lawrence and the Great Lakes and thence via the Lake of the Woods to the Mississippi. The British accepted the second alternative. The preliminary treaty was signed at Paris on 30 November 1782, not to become effective until France also made peace with Britain (Figure 3).

The treaty thus signed and, in due course, ratified by the parties was less favourable to the United States in three respects than the draft initialled on 5 October. It contained troublesome provisions for Loyalists and for British creditors, and the northern boundary followed the river and lake line instead of that by way of Lake Nipissing. By the latter change, the United States lost the greater and the most valuable part of the modern province of Ontario. Had Jay and Franklin been willing to treat with Oswald on the basis of his first commission, it is at least possible that they might have agreed upon Franklin's 'necessary terms' early in September, instead of a month later, and that Shelburne might have accepted these terms before he received news of the victory at Gibraltar.

What is remarkable about the treaty is that the United States got as much as it did, especially that the British surrendered title to all territory east of the Mississippi between the Great Lakes and the 31st parallel. For the explanation of this surrender, one must look neither to the legal weight of the colonial charters, nor to the military victories of George Rogers Clark, but to the enlightened policy of the Earl of Shelburne. Desirous of a peace treaty of

Diplomatic History

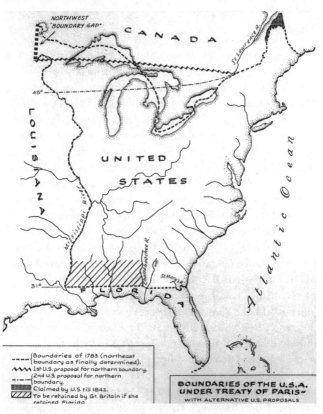

3. Map of the boundaries of the USA under the Treaty of Paris.

reconciliation, he saw a means of achieving it at small cost to the empire. The north-west, demanded by the Americans, appeared to him to be of slight value to Great Britain. The regulation of the fur trade in that area was proving ruinously expensive to the royal treasury, and experience had seemed to show that the region was of little value without control of the mouth of the Mississippi, now more firmly than ever in the hands of Spain. Why not buy American good will at so cheap a price?

The treaty

In detail, the principal provisions of the preliminary treaty signed on 30 November 1782 were as follows. The boundary of the United States began at the mouth of the St Croix River on the Maine frontier, followed that river to its source, and thence ran due north to the highlands dividing the St Lawrence from the Atlantic watershed, along those highlands to the north-westernmost head of the Connecticut River, and down that river to the 45th parallel, which it followed to the St Lawrence. It then followed the middle of the St Lawrence and of Lakes Ontario, Erie, and Huron, and connecting waters to Lake Superior; through that lake to Long Lake and then through certain small lakes and streams to the Lake of the Woods, from the north-westernmost point of which it was to be drawn due west to the Mississippi—an impossible line, since the Mississippi rose well to the southward. It followed the Mississippi down to the 31st parallel, ran due east along that parallel to the Chattahoochee, descended that stream to its junction with the Flint, leaped thence straight to the head of the St Mary's River, which it followed to the Atlantic. A secret article, introduced by the British but not incorporated in the final treaty, stipulated that if Great Britain retained West Florida, the northern line of that province should be, as it had been since 1764, not the 31st parallel but a line drawn east from the junction of the Yazoo with the Mississippi. The navigation of the Mississippi was to remain forever 'free and open to the subjects of Great Britain, and the citizens of the United States'.

Great Britain acknowledged the independence and sovereignty of the thirteen states individually, promised to withdraw all its armies, garrisons, and fleets from their soil and waters 'with all convenient speed', and conceded to American fishermen the 'liberty' to ply their trade much as before in the territorial waters of British North America. The United States, on its part, made certain promises in the interest of Loyalists and British creditors.

The parties agreed that creditors on either side should 'meet with no lawful impediment' in the recovery of the full value of bona fide debts previously contracted. The United States agreed that there should be no further prosecutions or confiscations of property against any persons for the parts they had taken in the war, and promised that it would 'earnestly recommend' to the legislatures of the states that, with certain exceptions, rights and properties of Loyalists be restored.

This preliminary treaty, minus the secret article, became the definitive treaty, signed 3 September 1783, at the time that Great Britain made peace with its other enemies. Great Britain ceded the Floridas, with limits undefined, to Spain, which was not a party to the treaty between Great Britain and the United States, and hence did not consider itself bound by its provisions with respect to the navigation of the Mississippi and the southern boundary of the United States. With both Spain and Great Britain, the United States still had many difficulties to overcome before the paper stipulations of the treaty could be converted into reality.

Problems of independence

Americans soon learned that independence was no bed of roses. When the war officially ended in 1783, the new government had been recognized by France, Great Britain, the Netherlands, and Sweden. Inexperienced diplomats from the United States had wandered over Europe in vain efforts to secure recognition from Russia, Prussia, Austria, Spain, and the Grand Duchy of Tuscany. In all these courts they had been coldly received. Few monarchs cared to imitate the indiscretion of Louis XVI of France, by countenancing rebellion and the institution of republican government.

A few other recognitions followed independence. In 1784, Spain finally gave in, sending Don Diego de Gardoqui as its first minister to the United States. Prussia made a treaty in 1785; Morocco in

1786. By 1787, then, the United States had commercial treaties with those two powers and with France (1778), the Netherlands (1782), and Sweden (1783). It had no commercial treaty with Great Britain until 1794; no treaty at all with Spain until 1795. The British government thought so little of the importance of the United States that, though it received John Adams as minister in 1785 and maintained consular or other agents in American ports, it did not send a fully-fledged minister to Philadelphia until 1791.

There were reasons for this temporary 'underprivileged' status of the United States. It was an upstart nation, the product of revolution, an experiment in democracy, small in population, and poor in fluid resources. But it also, under the Articles of Confederation, had a government that no foreign power need respect—a government without dependable revenue, without an army or navy, and without power to coerce the governments of the thirteen individual states. Such a government was unable to fulfil its obligations under the Treaty of Peace. Such a government could not make promises with assurance that they would be observed, or threats with any expectation that they would be carried out. Such a government was incapable of securing equality of commercial treatment abroad. It was incapable of enforcing its sovereignty in the area assigned to it by the Treaty of Peace or of putting an end, by either diplomacy or force, to foreign occupation of its soil. Not until after it was replaced by the more effective government provided for by the Constitution of 1787 were any of the pressing national problems solved. Even then, their solution owed much to the involvement of France, Spain, and Great Britain in the wars of the French Revolution. Then, to quote the familiar aphorism of Professor Samuel F. Bemis, 'Europe's distress became America's advantage.' The American diplomatic experience is a classic example of diplomacy in action, witnessing a major shift in the world's diplomatic landscape, while providing inspiration and template to other peoples and colonies on the cusp of modernity.

In Chapter 3 we will look at the impact of the diplomatic origins of the First World War, a European tragedy as well as the second most important historical event of the modern era. Diplomats of this era presided over the collapse of five empires—the Ottoman, the Austro-Hungarian, German, Italian, and Japanese—as well as the drastic decline of two major imperial systems, the British and the French. The Versailles system, together with the League of Nations, that followed, for all its promises, offered cold comfort to those who survived the Great War.

Chapter 3
Diplomatic origins of the Great War and Versailles

Sometimes it is difficult to believe, but the fifteen years before the outbreak of the First World War witnessed the heyday of the international peace movement. International peace societies became affluent and respectable, the Permanent Court of Arbitration was established at The Hague, and conciliation treaties were concluded in dozen lots. Some who lived through those calm and peaceful years believed, in all seriousness, that the days of war—at least major war—were in the past. It seemed clear that given the costly and destructive potentialities of modern technology, even victors in such a struggle would lose far more than they could possibly gain. Humankind, it was assumed, was a rational being and could see the folly of squandering precious resources in a game of self-destruction. Complaining of the costly European arms race of the era, German Social Democrat Eduard Bernstein wrote in 1893 that 'This continued arming, compelling the others to keep up with Germany, is a kind of warfare. I do not know whether this expression has been used previously, but one could say it is a cold war. . . . There is no shooting, but there is bleeding', in the sense of undermining the welfare of the peoples and the squandering of the resources needed in the work of social reform. Many thoughtful people had doubtless reached the same conclusion as British writer and future Nobel laureate Norman Angell, whose influential book, *The Great Illusion*, first published in the United Kingdom in 1909 under the title *Europe's Optical*

Illusion and republished in 1910, made a compelling case on the futility of war and obsolescence of militarism.

That all changed in the Bosnian capital of Sarajevo on 28 June 1914, when an assassination ignited a diplomatic crisis that culminated in a major world war. Gavrilo Princip, a young, ardent Serbian nationalist and member of a terrorist group, the Black Hand, mortally wounded Archduke Francis Ferdinand, heir to the Austro-Hungarian throne, and his wife Sophie. Since there was good reason to suspect Serbian involvement, the Austrian government decided to resolve the Balkan problem with violence, ending once and for all the constant threat to the stability of the multinational Hapsburg Empire. This was an area of vital interest to the Hapsburgs, because they feared unrest among their own Slavic population as well as Russian expansion. The Vienna government sent a legal expert to the scene to collect evidence in order to prepare a tight case. In July, the teenaged Princip and his fellow conspirators were placed on trial and were found guilty. When Belgrade failed to comply with Vienna's subsequent demands, Austria-Hungary declared war against Serbia on 28 July, and Belgrade was bombarded the next day.

Diplomatic origins of the First World War

Because of Europe's rival alliances and age-old ambitions and passions, the Great Powers soon found themselves engulfed in war, the veritable tidal wave produced by nationalism, imperialism, and militarism. Within days of Austria-Hungary's declaration of war, Imperial Germany (the other half of the Central Powers) declared war on Tsarist Russia, after the latter began general mobilization to defend Serbia; Germany declared war on France, after anticipating French support of Russia; and Great Britain declared war on Germany, after the German invasion of Belgium, whose neutrality Britain had long guaranteed. Japan came in as Britain's ally in the Far East, and Italy joined France and its allies (the Entente, or Allied Powers).

Eventually two dozen nations, including Turkey, Bulgaria, Romania, Greece, and, finally, America, in 1917, became immersed in the great struggle. German chancellor Otto von Bismarck's prediction that 'some damned foolish thing' in the Balkans would one day set off a general European war had proved correct. British statesman Sir Edward Grey also got it right when he said 'the lights are going out all over Europe, they will not be lit again in our lifetime'. He might just as well have included the next generation, as the events of 1914 paved the way for the next war, one continuous war, a new terrible Thirty Years War (Figure 4).

But it would be wrong, however, to imagine that the First World War, which resulted in the most extensive cultural devastation and mass killing in Europe since the Thirty Years War, was caused by a single assassination. Rather, its origins lay principally, though not

4. Trench warfare: *Oppy Wood* (1917), by John Nash.

exclusively, in the alliance diplomacy that had over many years developed between Germany, Austria, and Italy, on the one hand, and France and Russia, on the other. It was the entangling alliances that created the house of cards that when war broke out, or for that matter when the Russian Empire declared mobilization of its armies, collapsed, and the Great Powers—minus Italy, which held out for the highest bidder—went to war. The key to understanding this process—and German mentality on the eve of the First World War—necessarily begins with the rise of Prussia-Germany to Great Power status in the 19th century.

The unique role of the German officer corps

When one looks back over the history of the rise of Prussia-Germany to Great Power status in the 19th century, one sees that the achievement of the unification under Prussia was the consequence of three well-planned, short, sharp so-called cabinet wars (*Kabinettskriege*) designed and executed for very specific and limited aims. These were certainly not wars of conquest but rather for discrete political objectives, planned by the political leadership and carried out by highly professional generals. Behind these 19th-century achievements was the remarkable history of the rise of Prussia to European power status under the Hohenzollern electors and kings in the 17th and 18th centuries. It was they, particularly the King of Prussia from 1740 to 1786, Frederick the Great, who established the tradition of Prussian-German statecraft that rested on the correct relationship between the political leadership and the generals who served. This meant essentially that the King was responsible for all policy, and that if he decided that a war was necessary, for reasons of state, he commissioned the military to plan and execute it. In this way, it was understood that the maximum security of the country could be achieved. At all important levels, then, the Hohenzollern dynasty exerted a shaping influence on the formation of Prussian-German political culture that lasted until the end of the Second World War.

It should also be kept in mind that in a land-locked country like Prussia-Germany, with potential enemies on all sides, German statesmen would always have to reckon with the possibility of war at any time, and a permanent threat of attack, perhaps not tomorrow, but certainly sometime in the future. In that situation, the technical proficiency of the German officer corps was given the highest priority. Indeed, in Prussia-Germany, after the unification in 1871, one can observe a process evolving whereby the foreign policy priorities were governed by the army, which in the end came to dominate diplomacy.

The fateful permanence of Franco-German enmity

When German Chancellor Otto von Bismarck (Figure 5) founded the Reich in 1871, it was mainly at the expense of France in the third war of unification. France had been brutally humiliated, the emperor having been captured and sent into exile, the country suffering partial occupation, a massive war indemnity, and the loss of a major province, Alsace-Lorraine, which became a so-called *Reichsland* until the French retrieved it after the First World War. Such national shame meant that France had been turned into a permanent enemy of the new German Empire, and one had to expect it would want revenge. Bismarck was acutely aware of this and designed his diplomacy from that time forward on the assumption that France would always want to join with another major European power to keep Germany at bay and, at the right moment, to attack.

Much of the diplomatic history of this period at first revolves around this historic enmity between France and Germany and, specifically, over Alsace-Lorraine. And one can debate, as historians have, to what extent revenge permeated the ranks of French society. If it had been possible to ask people who France would go to war against—if they had had polls in those days—most people would probably have said Britain, not Germany. But the

5. Prince Otto von Bismarck.

spectre of that enmity was always there for Bismarck. Politically, then, the German chancellor had to head off the nightmare coalition against Germany, namely, France and Russia. Fearful of being attacked from both the east and west by France and Russia, the entire thrust of Bismarck's diplomacy was to maintain alliances as long as possible to delay the inevitable—the next war that was bound to happen sooner or later. Bismarck's concept was always to be 'a trios', to be three—always in a group of three powers aligned against France or, put another way, if there are five you want to be three. But there were basically two potential free agents: Italy, which would go to the highest bidder in 1915, and Great Britain. Nor was it a given that Great Britain would ally with France, its great enemy for centuries, or ally with Russia, because Great Britain and Russia had been fighting for a very long time in the 'Great Game', for control along places such as northern India, Pakistan, and all the way into South Asia.

In 1873, Bismarck cobbled together a pact between the three emperors of East/Central Europe: Prussia-Germany, Austria-Hungary, and Tsarist Russia. Concluded during a visit of the German chancellor to St Petersburg, the pact provided that if either party were attacked by another European power, the other would come to its assistance with 200,000 men. In short, Bismarck was trying to find a way to have two reliable friends. But this was going to prove extraordinarily difficult in the long term. Russia, especially, was not fully at ease with the arrangement. So, in 1879, Bismarck forged another kind of alliance between Germany and Austria-Hungary. Directed squarely against Russia, the Dual Alliance was predicated on German support for Austria-Hungary and Hungarian resistance against Russian activities in the Balkans. Concluded for five years, but regularly renewed, it remained in force until 1918 and was the foundation stone of Bismarck's alliance system.

The provisions were unequivocal: if either party were attacked by Russia, the other should come to its assistance with all forces; if either should be attacked by some other power, its partner should preserve at least neutrality; and if some other power should be supported by Russia, then each ally was obliged to aid the other. The Dual Alliance remained one of the continuities of the entire period, and explains why it was in July 1914 that the Germans gave the famous blank cheque to the Austrians after the assassination of Francis Ferdinand, allowing Vienna to do whatever it wanted to Serbia, knowing full well that it would eventually involve going to war with Russia.

The Reinsurance Treaty

As European politics developed in the 1890s, it was becoming increasingly clear that Bismarck's objective to sustain a reliable alignment of three powers was really not attainable, simply because the vital interests of Russia and Austria-Hungary could not be reconciled for long enough, particularly in the Balkans, which was perennially a source of friction and conflict. Bismarck then tried to stitch up one last deal with Russia in order to keep it in line with a separate and secret treaty called the Reinsurance Treaty in 1887, to replace the expiring Alliance of the Three Emperors (1881), which Russia refused to renew. Essentially, the two powers promised each other neutrality in the event of either becoming involved in war with a third power, but this was not to apply in case of *aggressive* war against France, or of Russia against Austria. They also were to work for the maintenance of the status quo in the Balkans, with Germany recognizing Russia's preponderant influence in Bulgaria. This famous treaty represented Bismarck's last effort to keep Russia from France and to buy its friendship by signing away things that he knew Russia could never get on account of Austrian opposition. But this proved unworkable, and the treaty lapsed formally after the German chancellor was retired in 1891.

It had become a dead letter before that. German historians have often tried to portray the Reinsurance Treaty as Bismarck's most brilliant concept because if it could have been kept alive, then France and Russia could not have entered into the military alliance they made in 1893. At that time, there was an exchange of notes between the Russian and French governments, formally accepting a military convention worked out eighteen months before. The agreement was political as much as military but classed as a military convention in order to circumvent the French constitution, which required submission of treaties to the chamber of deputies. The convention was to remain in force as long as the Triple Alliance (1892). It provided: that if France were attacked by Germany, or by Italy supported by Germany, Russia would supply all available forces against Germany; if Russia were attacked by Germany, or by Italy supported by Germany, France would supply all available forces against Germany. Moreover, and more ominously, in case the forces of the Triple Alliance, or of any one power member to it (Germany, Austria, and Italy), mobilized, France and Russia should mobilize without delay. While formal alliances were not published in *Figaro* or in *Le Temps*, or any other newspaper, everybody knew the rough outlines of the pact. The foreign ministries in London, in Vienna, in Berlin knew enough to know what the treaty meant: the diplomatic isolation of France had ended, and Bismarck's nightmare had become a reality.

The militarization of German diplomacy

In the post-Bismarck era of diplomacy, the Prussian-German general staff felt obliged from now on to prioritize the military solution to their diplomatic dilemma. They had already foreseen the eventuality of having to fight a two-front war against France in the west and Russia in the east, and had placed emphasis on strong defences in the east. However, under the new chief of the general staff, Count von Schlieffen, from 1891 to 1905, a revolutionary new concept took over, and it is important to dwell on it for a moment for what it reveals about the relationship between the military and the civilian government in the German Empire. The first thing to keep in mind is that German leadership believed in the inevitability of war with France, and whoever its allies might be. That was the only scenario they could imagine. Then, von Schlieffen came along and realized that the war would definitely have to be fought on two fronts, against France and Russia simultaneously. This posed a fundamental problem of logistics, but von Schlieffen had a solution to the problem.

It was based on a new concept—new for the modern era, anyway—called the 'war of annihilation' (*der Vernichtungskrieg*).

How was it supposed to work? Because Russia was so big and unwieldy and would take a long time to mobilize in the east, there would be a brief opportunity to destroy France, first in a lightning war (*Blitzkrieg*) that would be over in a few weeks, as in 1870, and then, having annihilated the French army, the German army could be turned eastward to bring the smaller holding army against Russia up to full strength in that sector. Superior German armament and planning would take care of the lumbering Russians in time for everybody to be home for Christmas. The concept bequeathed by von Schlieffen militarized German diplomacy even further.

What seems incredible, from today's standpoint, was that the civilian leadership, that is, the Chancellor and the cabinet, was not informed of crucial details. The most important one was that the plan in the west required the German army to march through neutral Belgium in order to be able as quickly as possible to get into position north of Paris to lay siege to the city. Another German army was simultaneously to drive across the Rhine, in the south, and envelop Paris from that direction. As stressed, it was meant to be over in two weeks, a 'super-Cannae', as von Schlieffen called it, in an allusion to the annihilation of Roman troops by Hannibal in 216 BC. And it nearly worked. So, what frustrated it? For one thing, Belgium refused to roll over, rejecting German demands that its armies be allowed to march through Belgium; indeed, the Belgian army fought bravely, even heroically, against overpowering military strength and savagery, including the summary execution of thousands of civilians as well as the calculated spoliation of the famous library of Louvain university and other historical sites. For another, and more important, the Schlieffen plan took no real account of the intervention of the British on behalf of Belgium, with whom they had a treaty dating from 1839 (the London Protocol). To be sure, von Schlieffen may have considered a British intervention, but he regarded it as a mere irritation, as though London could ever tolerate Belgium occupied by a potentially very hostile power. In his mind, the British could not fight a land war, a notion gleaned by their apparent dismal performance against the Boers in the South African War (1899–1902).

Looking back, one would have to say that von Schlieffen was at the very least basing his assessments on prejudice, because what actually frustrated his timetable from working out was the intervention of the British Expeditionary Force. The British ability to shoot rapid fire, a hard lesson learned of initial poor performance against the Boers, held up the German army, poised as it was in September 1914 to encircle Paris. The simple conclusion was that the decision to march through Belgium automatically involved Britain in the war on the side of France, and this fact resulted in the otherwise brilliant Schlieffen plan collapsing. But the point to remember is that it was both politically and militarily flawed to start with. After the war, in his memoirs, the German Chancellor Bethmann-Hollweg admitted as much. In fact, when he learned that the plan would set the British in motion, his nerve was effectively broken, and the real government of Germany devolved into the hands of the military.

The irrational continuation of the war of annihilation

Now that the plan had failed, the new commanding officer Erich von Falkenhayn, who replaced the younger Helmuth von Moltke, believed, or rather pretended to believe, he could still reach the original objective in the west and east, but the resources in men and materiel were simply not up to the gigantic task. Von Falkenhayn was really not himself totally certain he could bring it off. In early August, at the beginning of hostilities, he wrote: 'If in this undertaking we should be defeated, it was still a wonderful thing.' Expressed alternatively, he went on: 'We feel obliged to go through with this even though it will probably end in disaster.'

But it just got worse. Von Falkenhayn told the chancellor on 18 November 1914: 'So long as Russia, France and England hold together it will be impossible for us to bring off victory.' Indeed, von Falkenhayn would have preferred to make a separate peace with each of them, but he appreciated it was ruled out by the London Treaty of September 1914 that obliged the three allies to maintain a united front against Germany. It is hard to explain the mentality of the German leadership: on the one hand, it could grasp that pressing on could well to lead to a pointless catastrophe, but, on the other hand, it did not have the will to admit this openly. Germany's hatred of Britain would simply not allow it.

The anti-British thrust of German policy cannot be overstressed. In fact, the central German war aim in 1914–18 was the destruction of Great Britain and its empire, hence the frenetic energy and wealth expended on building a high seas fleet. Leading politicians and intellectuals saw Germany on the cusp of a great turning point in history that would lead to the establishment of Germany's ambition to become a global, rather than a European, power. The world would at last be free of the deadening hand of British commerce and intellectual mediocrity, and in its place would be established the enriching and edifying German cultural heritage. Rivalry with Britain, then, no less than enmity with France, drove German war planning.

Wartime diplomacy

All these ideas gained concrete expression in official government policy almost immediately after the war broke out. In a document only discovered in the Berlin archives after 1945 called the 'September Programme', the long-established aims of the German government were set out in detail. They were, in fact, the distillation of many memoranda already tabled in various ministries, and they foresaw the complete destruction of Russia and its empire in the east; similarly, the crushing of France and the occupation of large tracts of French territory in the east, so France could never again rise as an industrial power; the permanent occupation of Belgium, in particular for the purpose of establishing large naval bases on the English Channel from which to menace Britain. Holland, being a Germanic state with overseas territories, was to be bound to Germany in a special relationship. Specifically, the Dutch East Indies—present-day Indonesia—was to be made available to the German navy to allow the construction of powerful naval bases with which to hold down Britain's Pacific Dominions as well as India. The colonies of France, Belgium, and Portugal in Africa were to be ceded to Berlin—the so-called *Mittel Afrika* concept—with the French colonies in the Asia Pacific region to follow suit.

It is important to remember that the *Mittel Europa* grand design was actually implemented for a time after the defeat of Russia in 1918 in the famous Treaty of Brest-Litovsk, courtesy of Trotsky, Lenin, and the Bolshevik Revolution. Germany occupied all the territories from the Baltic Seas to the Black Sea, stripping Russia of its western colonies such as Courland, Poland, and the Ukraine. On the throne of all these countries, a prince of the various houses of the Eastern German principalities was to be installed. This treaty is historically important because it gives us a concrete image of what the future of Europe would have looked like in the event of German war plans coming together.

Ludendorff's last gamble

The euphoria among the German power elite after Brest-Litovsk was ecstatic. They now only had to conquer the Allied forces in the west, and this explains the massive offensives from the spring of 1918, when enormous reinforcements taken from the east to deploy on the Western Front went into action—and almost succeeded. On 21 March 1918, after a relatively brief bombardment of five hours, as opposed to the usual five days, 1.6 million German soldiers attacked the Allied defences in five separate offences over a front for forty miles. And they did break through. In five days, some German units had pushed more than forty miles, with a successful complementary attack taking place in Flanders. German forces had driven the British and French back almost to the English Channel. The Allies were fighting with their backs to the wall. What happened next was predictable and predicted, as the Germans once again began to outrun their cover and supplies, and began, at each one of these five points of German offensive, to encounter stiff resistance. Knowing that this was probably Germany's last chance to win the war, General Eric von Ludendorff ordered a last desperate attack, in July, in the Second Battle of the Marne. It was repulsed. The French, British, and now the Americans, who entered the war in April 1917, counterattacked, frustrating Ludendorff's plan for a great attack in Flanders, while enabling the newly appointed Commander-in-Chief of Allied armies in France, Ferdinand Foch, to take the initiative in the months ahead.

The Germans made one last, futile attempt to break the Allies' stand in France at the Battle of Amiens, where the Australians were used to make the crucial breakthrough at Saint-Quentin, thus making 8 August the blackest day for the German army. From then on, the German armies were rolled back until finally their generals called for an armistice that was signed on 11 November 1918, at 11 a.m. The war could not be won, although the German navy had decided after the armistice to break out into the Channel to stop reinforcements coming from England, believing that the German army would be able to keep the territory it still occupied in Belgium and France. This move by the admirals, in turn, provoked the German revolution on 15 November. The troops had had enough and had finally refused to be sacrificed for the impossible dreams of the officer corps and the German power elite. So erupted the 'November Revolution', which caused the

Kaiser and all the princes to abdicate. The outcome of the Revolution was that elections were called, after tedious negotiations of the various parties, and were held in January 1919. The new government under a republican constitution was compelled to sign the Treaty of Versailles on 28 June 1919, the fifth anniversary of that fateful day in Sarajevo.

A world safe for democracy

Principle was clearly lacking in the early years of the First World War. The British were confused about why they were fighting Germany. In 1908, Prime Minister David Lloyd George expressed the predominant view of Britain towards Germany:

> Here is Germany in the middle of Europe, with France and Russia on either side, and with a combination of greater armies than hers....Would we not be frightened, would we not build, would we not arm?

When London entered the war, it was, technically, in response to Germany's violation of Belgium's neutrality, though the original Treaty of London of 1839 left its signatories free to decide which course of action to pursue. Strictly speaking, then, Britain was under no obligation to go to war against Germany, though war was a legitimate option. Yet, even this was too slender to justify world war. Fully aware of this, Lloyd George attempted to expand the war aims to include independence for Poland and self-government for the nationalities of Austria-Hungary. Above all, this war must ensure a just and lasting peace. But it was American President Woodrow Wilson who provided the lofty ideals and honourable goals that rallied the Allies to fight the war. In his war address to the United States Congress in April 1917, he detailed in clear terms a rationale for fighting:

> We are glad, now that we see the facts with no veil of false pretence about them, to fight for the ultimate peace of the world and for the

liberation of peoples, the German peoples included: for the rights of nations great and small and the privilege of men everywhere to choose their way of life and of obedience. The world must be made safe for democracy. We have no selfish ends to serve. We desire no conquest, no dominion.…We are but one of the champions of the rights of mankind.

And there was more.

Wilson, with his acute sensitivity to the drift of history, saw a new era dawning—an era of responsibility, freedom, and, above all, peace. The League of Nations was to be the new tool for the new era. A partnership of democratic nations, it would be a league of honour, a partnership of opinion. Wilson was not aloof, however, to the sacrifices of war:

> It is a fearful thing to lead this great people into war, into the most terrible and disastrous of all war, civilization itself seeming to be in the balance. But the right is more precious than peace.…

The great departure in American diplomacy would have its price.

Fourteen Points

The war aims of the Allies were crowned by Wilson's 'Fourteen Points', which had been presented to Congress in January 1918. Among the issues stressed were open diplomacy, freedom of the seas, equality of trade conditions, reduction of armaments, adjustment of colonial claims, evacuation of Russia, Belgium, Alsace-Lorraine, Romania, and Serbia, and the establishment of an independent Polish state with access to the sea. The most important of the points was the last, which specified that a general association of nations would be formed to ensure the independence of nations. Wilson presented these principles as much to define the aims of the war as to define the terms of peace. While Germany, in agreeing to an armistice, accepted the

Fourteen Points, the Allies did not. Britain rejected the principle of freedom of the seas, while France demanded reparations for damages. At the same time, Wilson suffered a blow in his support at home in November 1918 when Republicans scored victories in congressional elections across the nation.

Under fire at home and abroad, Wilson felt he had to compromise. For example, he allowed Italy to seize Austria-Tyrol (though he did block their claim to Fiume), he gave Silesia and the Polish Corridor to Poland, and allowed Japan to take German territories in Shantung. While he prevented France from permanently seizing the Rhine, he shut his eyes to secret treaties dividing the spoils of the German Empire. Wilson was apparently willing to sacrifice provisions of the Fourteen Points in order to ensure the formation of the League of Nations. Whatever the faults of the Treaty of Versailles, Wilson was confident that they would be rectified by the League. Ironically, it was his own government—the US Senate—that ultimately killed American participation in the League and, with it, Wilson's hope for a new era of lasting peace, based on universal principles in place of great power manoeuvring.

Lloyd George also bent to pressure from his own countrymen to punish Germany. Winston Churchill would later recall Lloyd George's situation:

> The Prime Minister and his principal colleagues were astonished and to some extent overborne by the passion they encountered in the constituencies. The brave people whom nothing had daunted had suffered too much. Their unspent feelings were lashed by the popular press into fury. The crippled and mutilated soldiers darkened the streets. The returned prisoners told the hard tales of bonds and privation. Every cottage had its empty chair. Hatred of the beaten foe, thirst for his just punishment, rushed up from the heart of deeply injured millions.

Nor was Lloyd George as sympathetic to the Germans as Wilson. After all, Britain had suffered more than three million casualties (including nearly one million dead), while the United States suffered a little more than 300,000 casualties (including 115,000 dead). Defying Wilson's call for self-determination, Britain and the Dominions and France divided the German colonies among themselves after the war. Wilson could at most wrest a system of mandates, in which the colonial powers would deliver an annual account to the League.

Significantly, Lloyd George would not go as far as the French demanded. In a letter (referred to as the Fontainebleau Memorandum) to the American and French leadership, though directed at the latter, Lloyd George warned against creating new states containing large masses of German people and opposed continuing payment of reparations beyond the war generation. 'Our terms may be severe', he observed,

> they may be stern, even ruthless, but at the same time they can be so just that the country on which they are imposed will feel in its heart it has no right to complain. But injustice, arrogance, displayed in the hour of triumph will never be forgotten or forgiven.

It is doubtful that it had much impact on French thinking.

French revenge

The French, represented by 'the tiger', Georges Clemenceau, were the most vindictive of the powers represented at the Paris Peace Conference. More than the United States, Great Britain, and Italy, France had been devastated by the war. France had suffered more than four million casualties, including 1,385,000 dead. And this was not the first time France had been attacked by Germany. The French were still smarting from the Franco-Prussian War (1870–1), in which they had been crushed. In the peace that followed, Germany, it was well remembered, demanded that France pay an enormous war indemnity (five billion gold francs) and relinquish its border territory, Alsace-Lorraine. Thus, following France's victory in the First World War, Clemenceau naturally sought to cripple Germany militarily, politically, and economically, for vengeance and to prevent Germany from ever being a threat to France again.

In the end, it was the French who wielded the most influence on the Treaty of Versailles. France received back Alsace-Lorraine and acquired economic control of the coal-rich Saar territory, although the League would maintain political control of the formerly German region until a plebiscite was held in 1934.

France also took occupation for fifteen years of the German Rhineland, an industrial area along the French border. Three predominantly Polish-German provinces were given to the newly reconstructed state of Poland. The Allies also took land from Russia, which had broken from the Allies and declared a separate peace, to form new states. For the most part, however, the treaty-makers (Figure 6) were sensitive to the demands of ethnic groups in different areas for self-determination.

But the defeated Germans received no such considerations. The treaty detached the port of Danzig from Germany and made it a League 'free city', to give Poland access to the sea. It expressly forbade Austria—or what was left of it after the break-up of the Hapsburg Monarchy—to unite with Germany. It stripped the defeated nation of all its colonies. Germany was to have no heavy weapons, no air force, and no army over 100,000 men. Finally, and most controversially at the time—and significantly for the future—France and Britain levied on Germany reparations to cover the entire cost of the war, including such secondary expenses as pensions. Because the estimated sum was incalculable, the Allies left the exact amount open; yet there was no question

6. **The Big Four at Versailles—Woodrow Wilson, David Lloyd George, Georges Clemenceau, and Vittorio Orlando of Italy.**

Germany would be severely taxed. For openers, Germany was to give the Allies its entire merchant marine, all private property owned by its nationals in foreign countries, and large payments in cash and gold.

War guilt

As justification for the huge reparations' judgment—and in case anyone missed the point—the Allies included a punitive clause in the treaty. Article 231 reads:

> The Allied and Associated Governments affirm and Germany accepts the responsibility of Germany and her allies for causing all the loss and damage to which Allied and Associated Governments and their nationals have been subjected as a consequence of the war imposed on them by the aggression of Germany and her allies.

This held that despite the various causes of the war, despite the German peoples' repudiation of the Kaiser and the establishment of parliamentary democracy, the German people alone were to be held responsible—solely responsible—for the most destructive war in history.

Even before the Treaty of Versailles was signed, there were objections to it in Britain by a small minority of dissenters. Government opposition parties—Labour and Independent—criticized the document as fiercely political. A number of Labour Party members, indeed, had ties with the German working class, and decried what they believed was basically a punitive treaty. More significant was the eloquent and stinging critique published in 1919 by economist John Maynard Keynes (Figure 7), a former Treasury official and representative to the Paris Peace Conference, who resigned in protest at the treaty's economic terms. In *The Economic Consequences of the Peace*, Keynes denounced the treaty and its creators. He was kindest with Lloyd George who, he said, had decided on moderation too late. Wilson, on the other hand, he described as a pathetic figure who was 'ill informed', as well as 'slow and unadaptable'. 'He had no plan', complained Keynes, 'no scheme, no constructive ideas whatever for clothing with the flesh of life the commandments which he had thundered from the White House.' Keynes reserved most of his scorn, however, for Clemenceau, the man who viewed the affairs of Europe as 'a perpetual prize fight, of which France had won this round, but of which this round is certainly not the last'. According to Keynes, the French leader sought more than revenge from a wartime enemy—he sought the virtual destruction of a political and economic rival: 'He sees the issue in terms of France and Germany, not of humanity and of European civilization struggling forwards to a new order.' For Keynes, then, nothing less than the future of Europe was at stake.

The brunt of Keynes's argument was especially directed towards the reparations' clauses of the treaty. He took issue with the fact

7. John Maynard Keynes.

that no set amount was agreed upon. Never, he said, had a carte blanche been part of a treaty:

> It is evident that Germany's pre-war capacity to pay an annual foreign tribute has not been unaffected by the almost total loss of her colonies, her overseas connections, her mercantile marine, and her foreign properties, by the cession of ten percent of her territory and population, of one-third of her coal and of three quarters of her iron ore, by two million casualties amongst men in the prime of life,

by the starvation of her people for four years, by the burden of a vast war debt, by the depreciation of her currency to less than one-seventh of its former value, by the disruption of her allies and their territories, by Revolution at home and Bolshevism on her borders, and by all the unmeasured ruin in strength and hope of four years of all-swallowing war and final defeat.

Yet, continued Keynes, most estimates of a great indemnity from Germany rested on the false assumption that it would be possible for it to conduct in the future a vastly greater trade than it ever had in the past.

Keynes was also concerned that never had Britain levied such widely defined reparations. According to the treaty, the Reparations Commission was empowered to obtain $5 billion from Germany in any form (cash, property, raw materials) by May 1921. 'This provision', protested Keynes, 'has the effect of entrusting to the Reparations Commission for the period in question dictatorial powers over all German property of every description whatever.' But this appeared to be only the first payment of an enormous and unrealistic bill to the Allies. The former Treasury official also predicted a period of deep economic depression for Germany as a consequence of the treaty; millions would be unemployed, and many would die as the Weimar Republic's economy was strangled by Allied plans for peace. Indeed, it seemed to Keynes that the peacemakers had deliberately set out to destroy Germany: 'The economic clauses of the treaty are comprehensive, and little has been overlooked which might impoverish Germany now or obstruct her development in the future.' Finally, Keynes called attention to the fact that Germany's fate was intertwined with Europe's; with Germany crippled, the entire European economy would suffer. His official outlook was grim: 'An inefficient, unemployed, disorganized Europe faces us, torn by internal strife, and international hate, fighting, starving, pillaging, and lying.'

A mistake

Though his argument was exaggerated and later subject to revision, Keynes changed the drift of British opinion. His book ultimately destroyed British faith in the treaty, and the righteousness of the war itself, and unleashed a torrent of opposition to the peace terms. Where once they had felt the exultation and vengeance of victory, the British developed fear and guilt over what they had wrought. The British feared that the treaty's terms might cause themselves economic hardship. Moreover, London was now concerned with a new enemy, potentially more dangerous than Germany: the Soviet Union. Enforcement of the treaty, the British worried, might even drive Germany into the arms of the Bolsheviks. In addition, many in Britain had moral qualms about the treaty. Keynes had given them misgivings about taking territory from Germany, while demanding reparations for the cost of the war. Was it right to impose such hardships on a country already devastated by war? The British had traditionally been more forgiving. The intensity of French vindictiveness made many sympathetic towards the Germans. Of course, the Germans sought to exploit these emotions by launching a massive propaganda campaign in Great Britain. While it did have an effect, it only heightened the already strong doubts about the morality of the terms of peace. Within a generation, even many in France came to the same conclusion.

Beyond the specific provisions of the treaty, the underlying principle of the peace—that Germany was solely responsible for the outbreak of the war—increasingly disturbed the British. Many believed that neither Germany nor any other nation caused the war, but that it was a spontaneous action by all those involved. Fourteen years after he had negotiated the terms of the Treaty of Versailles, David Lloyd George argued that the First World War was a mistake:

I am convinced after a careful perusal of all the documents available on all sides that the Kaiser never had the remotest idea he was plunging—or being plunged—into a European war.... He was not anticipating a costly war but a cheap diplomatic triumph.

In the end, the negotiations were botched by everybody engaged in directing them. For the former Prime Minister: 'War ought to have been, and could have been averted.' By 1937, few in Europe and even America disagreed. Diplomacy had failed.

The diplomatic history of the First World War left an indelible mark on the 20th century, as Western politicians, policymakers, and diplomats experienced the disillusionment of the Versailles system and the folly of appeasement, struggled through the Great Depression, witnessed the rise of Communism, Fascism, and Nazism, and recoiled from the West's abandonment of Czechoslovakia to Hitler at Munich in 1938. The Munich Conference, featuring Hitler and British Prime Minister Neville Chamberlain, proved a spectacular failure in summit diplomacy. In contrast, the summit meeting of Soviet leader Joseph Stalin and British Prime Minister Winston Churchill in Moscow in December 1944, discussed in Chapter 4, was a huge success and premier example of diplomacy in action.

Chapter 4
The night Stalin and Churchill divided Europe

Of the many fascinating episodes that punctuate the diplomacy of the Second World War, few have intrigued scholars more than the secret Balkan spheres-of-action agreement worked out by Prime Minister Winston Churchill and Marshal Joseph Stalin at the Anglo-Soviet conference (British code-named TOLSTOY) held in Moscow in the autumn of 1944. It was late in the evening of 9 October. In his first encounter with Stalin since the meeting of the Big Three at Tehran in 1943 (Figure 8), Churchill, believing 'the moment...apt for business', appealed to the Soviet dictator in the simple language of power politics: 'Let us settle about our affairs in the Balkans.' Specifically, he went on:

> We have interests, missions, and agents there. Don't let us get at cross-purposes in small ways. So far as Britain and Russia are concerned, how would it do for you to have ninety per cent dominance in Rumania, for us to have ninety per cent of the say in Greece, and go fifty-fifty about Yugoslavia?

In the time this was being translated, the British leader recalled in his memoirs:

> I wrote on a half-sheet of paper—
> Rumania
> Russia 90 per cent

The others 10 per cent

Greece

Great Britain (in accord with USA) 90 per cent

Russia 10 per cent

Yugoslavia 50–50 per cent

Hungary 50–50 per cent

Bulgaria

Russia 75 per cent

The others 25 per cent

In the presence of the small gathering that had come together that night in the Kremlin, Stalin looked on, listening for the translation. Having finally understood, he paused slightly and 'took his blue pencil and made a large tick upon it, and passed it back to us'. Thus, concluded Churchill, 'It was all settled in no more time than it takes to set down.' With only minor variations—80 per cent–20 per cent predominance in favour of the Soviets in Hungary and Bulgaria, reached by Foreign Secretary Anthony Eden and Minister for Foreign Affairs Vyacheslav Molotov, in two additional meetings amidst resolution of the tangled Bulgarian armistice dispute—the original agreement remained intact, or so it was thought.

Upon his return to London, the Prime Minister reported confidently to the House of Commons that, so far as the Balkans was concerned, he and Stalin had been able to reach complete agreement. Moreover, he added,

> I do not feel there is any immediate danger of our combined war effort being weakened by divergence of policy or of doctrine in Greece, Rumania, Bulgaria, Yugoslavia and, beyond the Balkans, Hungary. We have reached a very good working arrangement about all these countries, singly and in combination, with the object of concentrating all their efforts, and concerting them with ours against the common foe, and providing, as far as possible, for a peaceful settlement.

8. The Big Three at Tehran in 1943—Stalin, Franklin D. Roosevelt, and Churchill.

Though it is commonly agreed that the subject of Balkan percentages was not again officially raised at Yalta, in February 1945—or at any other time during the remainder of the Second World War—historians continue to debate the significance of the personal diplomacy concluded at TOLSTOY, the most important of the wartime conferences.

Churchill's 'need of another personal meeting with Stalin'

What prompted Churchill to travel to Moscow in October 1944 in search of a Balkan agreement? Few scholars have had any reason to doubt the Prime Minister's own account of his decision to embark on this journey. Against the background of the aftermath of the Allied operation (Overlord) that launched the successful invasion of Nazi-occupied Western Europe in June 1944 and the

Soviet offensive of the summer of 1944, which witnessed the occupation of Bucharest and a declaration of war against Bulgaria, to be followed shortly by an armistice, Churchill 'felt the need of another personal meeting with Stalin, whom I had not seen since Teheran [in 1943], and with whom, in spite of the Warsaw tragedy, I felt new links since the successful opening of "Overlord"'.

The Prime Minister observed furthermore that, while 'the arrangements which I had made with the President in the summer to divide our [Anglo-Soviet] responsibilities for looking after particular countries [Greece and Romania, respectively] affected by the movements of the armies had tided us over the three months for which our arrangement ran', the time had come to rethink the agreement anew. The first Balkan agreement, so called, originated with the British leader's concern in early May that something had to be done to put the Russians in their place. 'I am not very clear on it myself', the Prime Minister minuted Eden on 4 May, 'but evidently we are approaching a showdown with the Russians about their Communist intrigue in Italy, Yugoslavia and Greece....I must say their attitude becomes more difficult every day.' Initially, Churchill requested that the Foreign Minister draft a paper 'for the Cabinet and possibly for the Imperial Conference setting forth shortly,...the brute issues between us and the Soviet Government which are developing in Italy, in Rumania, in Bulgaria, in Yugoslavia and above all in Greece'.

For Churchill, the issue was unequivocal: 'Are we going to acquiesce in the Communization of the Balkans and perhaps of Italy?' The paper, which was placed before the War Cabinet on 7 June, suggested that an effort ought to be made 'to focus our [British] influence in the Balkans by consolidating our position in Greece and Turkey...and, while avoiding any direct challenge to Russian influence in Yugoslavia, Albania, Rumania and Bulgaria, to avail ourselves of every opportunity in order to spread British influence in those countries'. Even while the paper was being drafted, Eden sought out the Soviet Ambassador in London in order to establish the Balkan ground rules.

On 5 May, only a day after Churchill had minuted his concern, Eden called on Soviet Ambassador Gousev and raised

> the possibility of our agreeing between ourselves as a practical matter that Rumanian affairs would be in the main the concern of the Soviet Government, while Greek affairs would be in the main our concern, each Government giving the other help in the respective countries.

Less than two weeks later, the Soviets replied to the suggestion positively with the proviso, to quote Eden's cable to his ambassador in Moscow, that,

> before giving any final assurance in the matter, they would like to know whether we had consulted the United States Government and whether the latter also agreed to this arrangement. If so, the Soviet Government would be ready to give us a final affirmative answer.

The Foreign Secretary's final remarks are instructive:

> I [Eden] said that I did not think we had consulted the United States Government in the matter but would certainly be ready to do so. *I could not imagine that they would dissent.* After all, the matter was really related to the military operations of our respective forces. Rumania fell within the sphere of the Russian armies and Greece within the Allied Command under General Wilson in the Mediterranean. Therefore it seemed natural that Soviet Russia should take the lead in Rumania and we in Greece, and that each should support the other.

Inasmuch as it was common knowledge that the old Wilsonian Secretary of State Cordell Hull was, in fact, flatly opposed to any division of Europe or section of Europe into spheres of influence—or, to paraphrase his comments to Congress upon his return from the Foreign Ministers' conference at Moscow in late 1943, 'any other of the special arrangements through which, in the unhappy past, the nations strove to safeguard their security or to promote their interests'—it is in itself hard to imagine how Eden ever expected to carry the Americans along. It is also tempting to think that the Kremlin had deliberately nudged the Foreign Secretary into a trap.

In any case, the British Ambassador Lord Halifax called on Hull on 30 May to broach the subject. Concealing the fact that Eden had already spoken to the Soviet Union, and representing the suggestions as the fruit of the Foreign Secretary's 'own independent reflection', Halifax inquired how the United States 'would feel about an arrangement between the British and the Russians to the effect that Russia might have a controlling influence in Rumania and Great Britain a controlling influence in Greece'. Though promising to give the matter serious attention, Hull voiced deep reservations about the wisdom of abandoning 'the fixed rules and policies which are in accord with our broad basic declarations of policy, principles and practice'. Before receiving Halifax's report of his meeting with Hull, and still anticipating no difficulty in the State Department, Eden requested the Prime Minister to send a personal message to Roosevelt in order to 'reinforce' the Foreign Office's representations to Hull. It was at this juncture, however, that Churchill and Eden crossed signals, raising serious doubts, at least in some American minds, as to the true aims of British policy in the Balkans.

Secret revealed

After observing that there had 'recently been disquieting signs between ourselves and the Russians in regard to the Balkan countries and in particular Greece', Churchill let the proverbial cat out of the bag when he told FDR that:

[W]e therefore suggested to the Soviet Ambassador here that we should agree between ourselves as a practical matter that the Soviet Government would take the lead in Rumanian affairs, while we would take the lead in Greek affairs, each Government giving the other help in the respective countries.

In asking Roosevelt to give this proposal his 'blessing', the Prime Minister took pains to point out to the election-bound President that:

We do not of course wish to carve up the Balkans into spheres of influence and in agreeing to the arrangement we should make it clear that it applied only to war conditions and did not affect the rights and responsibilities which each of the three Great Powers will have to exercise at the peace settlement and afterwards in regard to the whole of Europe.

The thrust of this was repeated to Halifax a week later. In the meantime, Halifax conveyed to Eden his only reason for concealing Whitehall's initiative in approaching the Soviets first: 'I purposely did not disclose the fact that you had already taken the matter up with the Russians', he cabled Eden on 5 June, 'because, I thought, we were more likely to get the Americans along with us in that way'. Furthermore, he went on to remonstrate:

Subject to what you and the Prime Minister may feel and to obvious necessities of urgency that may arise, it would seem wise, when you have instructed me to take up something with Mr Hull, to defer action through the higher channel of the President until I have been able to report progress with Mr Hull, and further action that you may wish to take can be taken with the knowledge of what has passed at lower level. Otherwise we risk confusion and embarrassment.

Halifax got both for his trouble.

After some debate in State between the European and Near Eastern Desks, Acting Secretary of State Edward Stettinius handed the file over to Assistant Secretary of State Breckenridge Long for a recommendation. During the next several days, Long prepared an answer in the negative, which in turn was approved without change by the President on 10 June. Roosevelt advised Churchill in no uncertain language that his government was 'unwilling to approve the proposed arrangement'. Washington's position was as follows:

> Briefly, we acknowledge that the militarily responsible Government in any given territory will inevitably make decisions required by military developments but are convinced that the natural tendency for such decisions to extend to other than military field would be strengthened by an agreement of the type suggested. On our opinion, this would certainly result in the persistence of differences between you and the Soviets and, in the division of the Balkans into spheres of influence despite the declared intention to limit the arrangements to military matters.

What to offer in its place? 'We believe', the President gently lectured the Prime Minister, 'efforts should preferably be made to establish consultative machinery to dispel misunderstandings and restrain the tendency toward the development of exclusive spheres.' Though, to be sure, without any risk of disturbing his special relationship with Roosevelt, Churchill replied with a forcefulness of his own.

'Action is paralysed', he cabled the same day, 'if everybody is to consult everybody else about everything before it is taken. The events will always outstrip the changing situation in these Balkan regions.' Besides which, 'Somebody must have the power to plan and act'; consultative machinery 'would be a mere obstruction, always overridden in any case of emergency by direct interchange between you and me, or either you and Stalin.' Explaining the realities of the prospect of Soviet troops on Romanian soil—'they will probably do what they like anyhow'—and the British investment of both blood and treasure in Greece, Churchill appealed to the President's vanity with several questions: 'Why is all this effective direction to be broken up into a committee of mediocre officials such as we are littering about the world? Why can you and I not keep this in our hands considering how we see eye to eye about so much of it?' In conclusion, the Prime Minister proposed that the President agree to a trial period of three months, although clearly, it seems, Churchill would have settled for two months as preferable to nothing. Roosevelt was apparently impressed with the Prime Minister's logic. For, without notifying State for over two weeks that he had reversed course, the President acquiesced in Churchill's proposal, with the provision, '[W]e must be careful to make it clear that we are not establishing any postwar spheres of influence.' Churchill, who doubtless must have congratulated himself both on his power of persuasion and his ability to override the State Department, was grateful. All that remained was to pass on the information to the Soviets.

'The United States Government have now been consulted', Eden wrote to the Soviet Ambassador in London on 19 June, 'and they agree with the arrangement proposed.' More to the point, the Secretary noted, 'They feel some anxiety, however, lest it should extend beyond the immediate circumstances for which it has been devised and should lead to the partition of the Balkan countries into spheres of influence', a prospect at variance with London's intentions 'that the arrangement should apply only to war conditions and should not affect the rights and responsibilities which each of our three Governments will have to exercise at the peace settlement and afterwards in regard to the whole of Europe'. In any case, he finished in a manner intimating only a hint of disagreement:

> In order to guard against any danger of the arrangement extending
> beyond the purpose for which it has been devised we have
> suggested to the United States Government, and they have agreed,

that it should be given a trial of three months after which it would
be reviewed by our three Governments. I hope, therefore, that the
Soviet Government will agree to the arrangement coming into force
on this basis.

The Soviet Government had other plans, however. Ambassador
Gousev replied on 8 July that in light of changed circumstances,
particularly certain apprehensions expressed by the United States,
the Kremlin would consider it necessary to give the question
further consideration. Moreover, he added, 'the Soviet
Government deem it advisable to make a direct approach to the
United States Government in order to obtain more detailed
information as to their attitude to this question'. This was done on
1 July. Moscow had called Eden's bluff.

The State Department, with Hull back in the picture and the
President in the midst of an election campaign, replied to the
Soviet request two weeks later, on 15 July, observing that 'It is
correct that the Government of the United States assented to the
[Balkan] arrangement, for a trial period of three months, this
assent being given in consideration of present war strategy.' This
particular 'overriding consideration' aside, State continued, the
United States

> would wish to make known its apprehension lest the proposed
> agreement might, by the natural tendency of such arrangements,
> lead to the division, in fact, of [the] Balkan region into spheres of
> influence, [which] would be an unfortunate development, in view
> of decisions of Moscow Conference…

As a consequence of those decisions, State had hoped that no
projected measure would

> be allowed to prejudice efforts towards direction of policies of the
> Allied governments along lines of collaboration rather than
> independent action, since any arrangement suggestive of spheres of

influence cannot but militate against establishment and effective functioning of a broader system of general security in which all countries will have their part.

Still—no doubt with due respect to the President's previous determination to do otherwise—the Secretary of State let it be known that he would have no particular objection to a three months' trial period so long as Anglo-Soviet actions in no way affected 'the rights and responsibilities which each of the three principal allies will have to exercise during the period of re-establishment of peace and afterwards in regard to the whole of Europe'. And, finally, in case anyone missed the point, State went on notice in assuming aloud 'that the arrangement would have neither direct or indirect validity as affecting interests of this Government or of other Governments associated with the three principal allies'. In addition to the arguments against spheres of influence contained in this memorandum, there were other, perhaps less lofty, considerations to be taken into account.

In a top-secret letter written to Hull in May 1944, Admiral William D. Leahy, Roosevelt's chief of staff, advanced a number of military arguments in opposition to spheres of influence along the lines of the proposed Anglo-Soviet agreement. According to Leahy, whose diary records that he did 'not intend to sacrifice American soldiers and sailors in order to impose any government on any people, or to adjust political differences in Europe or Asia, except to act against an aggressor with the purpose of preventing an international war', the nation's best interests post-war would be served by maintaining 'the solidarity of [the] three great powers', until such time as 'arrangements will be perfected for the prevention of world conflicts'. Furthermore, and as any world conflict in the foreseeable future would most likely find Britain and Soviet Russia in opposite camps, with Moscow in an overwhelmingly dominant military position on the continent, about which the United States could presently do little, it would be prudent for America to 'exert its utmost efforts and utilize all its influence to prevent such a situation arising and to promote a spirit of mutual cooperation between Britain, Russia and ourselves'.

Put another way, Leahy was saying that in the case of war between London and Moscow, probably occasioned by a territorial dispute on the continent,

> we might be able to successfully defend Britain [proper], but we could not, under existing conditions, defeat Russia....we would find ourselves [therefore] engaged in a war which we could not win even though the United States would be in no danger of defeat and occupation.

To attempt to eschew such a situation was simply to recognize one of the new international facts of life:

> the recent phenomenal development of the heretofore latent Russian military and economic strength—a development which seems certain to prove epochal in its bearing on future politico-military international relationships, and which has yet to reach the full scope with Russian resources.

While it is doubtful that Leahy's remarks represented a significant reversal of the nation's official attitude towards balance-of-power politics, they are significant in the sense that they indicate an official awareness of the limits of American power to influence events in post-war continental Europe, including the Balkans.

FDR's disapproval

Meanwhile, President Roosevelt expressed his strong disapproval of the manner in which the British had handled the proposed Balkan arrangement. 'I think I should tell you frankly', FDR cabled Churchill on 22 June, 'that we were disturbed that your people took this matter up with us only after it had been put up to the Russians and they had inquired [at this late juncture] whether we were agreeable'. More or less accepting the Foreign Office's explanation 'that the proposal "arose out of a chance remark" which was converted by the Soviet Government into a formal proposal', the President hoped that 'matters of this importance can be prevented from developing in such a manner in the future'. The Prime Minister was quick to reply, pointing out in addition to the long-belaboured observations that the Soviets were the only power that could do anything in Romania and that the Greek burden rested almost entirely on the British, that he had had no complaints of Roosevelt's recent private messages to Stalin with regard to the Poles. 'I am not complaining at all of this', he assured the President, 'because I know we are working for the general theme and purposes and I hope you will feel that this has been so in my conduct of the Greek affair.'

Appealing to FDR's political instincts, the Prime Minister conceded that, 'It would be quite easy for me, on the general principle of slithering to Left, which is so popular in foreign policy, to let things rip when the King of Greece would probably be forced to abdicate' and the Communist-led elements 'would work a reign of terror'; accordingly, the only way to prevent such a state of affairs was to persuade Moscow to quit boosting the Communists 'and ramming it forward with all their force'. It was in these circumstances, he concluded, 'I proposed to the Russians a temporary working arrangement for the better conduct of the war. This was only a proposal and had to be referred to you for agreement.' Roosevelt seems to have grasped the message when several days later he replied to the Prime Minister, saying, 'It appears that both of us have inadvertently taken unilateral action in a direction that we both now agree to have been expedient for the time being.' Nonetheless, he made clear, 'It is essential that we should always be in agreement in matters bearing on our allied war matters.' The incident seemed closed.

Several weeks later, upon receipt of news from Eden that the Kremlin had now found it necessary to give the question of a Balkan division 'further consideration' and was, in fact, approaching the United States direct, Churchill virtually went through the ceiling. 'Does this mean', he minuted the Foreign Secretary on 9 July:

> that all we had settled with the Russians now goes down through the pedantic interference of the United States, and that Rumania and Greece are to be condemned to a regime of triangular telegrams in which the United States and ourselves are to interfere with the Russian treatment of Rumania, and the Russians are to boost up E.A.M. [the National Liberation Front] while the President pursues a pro-King policy in regard to Greece, and we have to make all things go sweet? If so, it will be a great disaster.

The following day, 10 July, Eden informed the War Cabinet that the proposed Anglo-Soviet spheres-of-action agreement regarding Greece and Romania had, in the Foreign Secretary's words, 'broken down'.

Puzzled by the actual meaning of State's response to the Soviet inquiry of 1 July—'Does this mean that the Americans have agreed to the three months' trial, or is it all thrown in the pool again?—and increasingly concerned by the prospect of Soviet interference in Greek affairs, particularly the unheralded dispatch of a mission of Russian officers there in late July, Churchill would have to await the changing tides of war before making another approach to the USSR on a Balkan settlement. Moreover, in the light of past experience with the Americans, it is hardly surprising that the next time the Prime Minister sought to play his hand in the Balkans, he would approach Stalin himself, a man with whom Churchill 'considered one could talk as one human being to another'. Until such time, and for all intents and purposes, the May Agreement had all but become a dead letter.

By October 1944, the Prime Minister's time had come. For better and for worse, the war situation had fundamentally been altered since spring. With respect to the latter, the Red Army had firmly established itself in Romania and Bulgaria and had only recently penetrated Yugoslavia and Hungary; by the same token, British influence in the region had been confined to Greece and Yugoslavia, principally in the form of military liaison missions with the guerrilla organizations of those countries and, to a lesser extent, by hosting the Greek and Yugoslav governments in exile. Of urgency to Churchill was the threat to Greece posed by the possible Bulgarian retention of parts or all of Macedonia and Thrace occupied during the course of the war. The fact that Bulgaria now marched on the side of the Allies proved cold comfort indeed, considering the Soviets were calling the tune.

All of this is not to say, however, that Churchill would be travelling to Moscow without some bargaining power of his own. For, if the Russians had made great advances in south-eastern Europe, the Western Powers had also won remarkable victories. Since May, the Second Front had been established, Paris and Brussels had both been liberated, and the frontier of the Reich breached. In fact, it began to appear that it might well be the Western half of the Grand Alliance that would reach Berlin first before the advancing Red Army. Furthermore, the Prime Minister could well boast that, at least until July 1944, the British Empire had more men in contact with the enemy the world over than had the United States. Add to this Churchill's natural tendency, as he cabled Stalin on 4 October, to return to Moscow under the much happier conditions created since August 1942, at which time it had been the Prime Minister's sober mission to apprise the great Soviet leader that there would be no Second Front in 1942. The great remaining question facing Churchill was, to paraphrase Halifax's words of the previous June, how 'to get the Americans along with us'. Predictably enough, the Prime Minister went straight to the President, with whom he had just experienced the most cordial relations at the Second Quebec Conference (11–19 September) and at Hyde Park, American resistance to eleventh-hour Balkan military operations to the contrary notwithstanding.

On 29 September, Churchill advised FDR that he and Eden were considering flying to Moscow, the two great objects of the exercise being, 'first, to clinch his [Stalin's] coming in against Japan and, secondly, to try to effect a friendly settlement with Poland. There are other points too about Greece and Yugoslavia which we could also discuss.' And lest there be any misunderstanding, the Prime Minister reassured the President, '[W]e should keep you informed of every point.' Churchill followed up several days later, requesting Roosevelt to send Stalin a message, saying that he had approved of the mission, and that the US Ambassador in Moscow would be available to take part in the proceedings. The Prime Minister again wanted the President's blessing, and almost got it.

In a draft reply prepared by Admiral Leahy, and approved without change by the White House, Roosevelt 'merely wished Churchill "good luck", saying he understood perfectly why the trip had to be made'. At this point, according to Robert Sherwood, presidential adviser Harry Hopkins, having 'learned that Roosevelt was dispatching a cable to Churchill in which he...in effect wash[ed] his hands of the whole matter [Balkans], with the implication that he was content to let Churchill speak for the United States as well as for Great Britain', intercepted the message and directed that it not be sent, albeit a decision made after Hopkins had phoned FDR. Sensitive both to Ambassador Averell Harriman's September warnings from Moscow that the time had come to make clear to the Soviets 'what we expect of them as the price of our good will' and to Churchill's well-known inclination to make a Balkan deal, Hopkins persuaded Roosevelt it would be a mistake to send vague messages to Churchill and Stalin which would probably have the opposite effect of detaching the administration from the results of their meeting—whether on the Polish, Balkan, or any other controversial issue. With the elections a month away and having just burned his fingers with the so-called Morgenthau

Plan, to punish Germany severely, the President agreed to send Churchill and Stalin a different kind of message.

'I can well understand the reasons why you feel that an immediate meeting between yourself and Uncle Joe [Stalin] is necessary before the three of us can get together,' FDR responded to Churchill on 4 October. 'The questions which you will discuss there', he continued, 'are ones which are, of course, of real interest to the United States, as I know you will agree. I have therefore instructed Harriman to stand by and to participate as my observer, if agreeable to you and Uncle Joe, and I have so informed Stalin.' Finally, the President concluded unequivocally, 'While naturally Averell [Harriman] will not be in a position to commit the United States—I could not permit any one to commit me in advance—he will be able to keep me fully informed and I have told him to return to me as soon as the conference is over.' All in all, the meeting in Moscow should prove 'a useful prelude' to another meeting with the Big Three after the elections. Churchill replied the next day, thanking Roosevelt for his thoughts on the matter and for his good wishes.

Inasmuch as it was now apparent that he would not be receiving Roosevelt's blessing in advance, the Prime Minister then sought to protect his own freedom of manoeuvre: 'I am very glad that Averell [Harriman] should sit in at all principal conferences; but you will not I am sure, wish this to preclude private tête-à-têtes between me and UJ [Stalin] or Anthony [Eden] and Molotov, as it is often under such conditions that the best progress is made', though he went on to reassure the President once again that 'you can rely on me to keep you constantly informed of everything that affects our joint interests apart from the reports Averell will send'.

Roosevelt's message to Stalin, who seemed puzzled by it all, having supposed Churchill was coming in accordance with agreements reached at Quebec, expressed similar sentiments with regard to the Prime Minister's wishes to have an early conference and

similar instructions with regard to allowing Ambassador
Harriman to stand in as his observer. Perhaps preoccupied more
with preserving his options in future than he ought to have been,
the President underscored his personal concern with the coming
talks. 'You, naturally, understand', he observed,

> that in this global war there is literally no question, political or
> military, in which the United States is not interested. I am firmly
> convinced that the three of us, and only the three of us, can find the
> solution to the still unresolved questions. In this sense, while
> appreciating the Prime Minister's desire for the meeting, I prefer to
> regard your forthcoming talks with Churchill as preliminary to a
> meeting of the three of us, which so far as I am concerned, can take
> place any time after the elections here.

Again, the British had failed to carry the Americans along in
advance, but this time there would be absolutely no doubt, both in
Moscow and London, where the United States stood.

Interestingly, the very diplomat who had assisted in the drafting of
these messages to Stalin and Churchill, Charles E. Bohlen, Chief
of the Division of Eastern European Affairs, was simultaneously
pressing for an unequivocal statement of the administration's
position in the Balkans, in the absence of which Washington
would only have itself to blame for any subsequent
misunderstanding. 'This Government', he contended in State,
'[was] to some extent at fault because neither of our principal
allies had yet a clear picture as to what the US will do and how
much responsibility it will assume in Eastern Europe.'
Furthermore, Bohlen indicated that inasmuch as the Soviets
tended to be more inclined to 'accept comprehensive plans
presented to them by others' rather than draw up their own,
perhaps the time had come to raise 'the question as to whether we
might not present to the Russians a plan for dealing with this
area'. By this time, however, Churchill was already in Moscow
presenting a plan of his own.

Stalin 'ready to discuss anything'

At the outset of his meeting with Stalin on the evening of 9 October, Churchill had 'hoped they might clear away many questions about which they had been writing to each other for a long time', to which Stalin replied 'that he was ready to discuss anything'. Turning from a discussion of the Polish Question, whose ramifications would ultimately dominate the conference proceedings until the departure of the British delegation on 18 October, Churchill declared, 'Britain must be the leading Mediterranean Power and…hoped Marshal Stalin would let him have first say about Greece in the same way as Marshal Stalin [would have the first say] about Rumania.' Without once alluding to the May Agreement, Stalin concurred, pointing out that 'if Britain were interested in the Mediterranean then Russia was equally interested in the Black Sea'. It was further agreed that the two powers should share equal interests in Hungary and Yugoslavia.

The sticking point, however, was Bulgaria, which posed the single greatest threat to the British position in Greece. According to the records of the meeting, 'The Prime Minister suggested that where Bulgaria was concerned the British interest was greater than it was in Rumania', where London's influence on the Soviet-controlled Allied Control Commission was admittedly nominal. Stalin, who suggested that the Prime Minister claimed too much for Britain in the area, countered that Bulgaria was after all a Black Sea country and, by extension, a matter of Russian concern. In response to Stalin's query, 'Was Britain afraid of anything?', Eden, who until now had remained silent, retorted 'that Britain was not afraid of anything'. He also reminded the Soviet leader 'that Britain had been at war with Bulgaria for three years [in contrast to recent Soviet–Bulgarian belligerency] and wanted a small share of the control of that country'. The Bulgarian armistice issue, together with a change in the ratio of Soviet predominance in Hungary (80 per cent–20 per cent), was eventually settled by Eden and Molotov in the course of discussion over the next two days. Thus, a bargain of sorts had been struck over a division of Anglo-Soviet responsibilities in the Balkans; what it meant, exactly, was of course another matter.

From another level of analysis, it is interesting to note the missing President's influence on the participants' manoeuvrings. When it came to phrasing the division of responsibilities, Churchill, with the recent American experience fresh in his mind, thought it 'better to express these things in diplomatic [more euphemistic] terms and not to use the phrase "dividing into spheres", because the Americans might be shocked'. Still, 'as long as he and the Marshal understood each other he could explain matters to the President', no doubt at a time and place of the Prime Minister's choosing.

At this juncture, Stalin interrupted his guest 'to say that he [too] had received a message from President Roosevelt', indicating FDR's desire both to have the American Ambassador stand in as his observer and to regard the talks themselves as of a preliminary nature. Lest Stalin arrive at a false impression, Churchill advised the Soviet leader that he of course agreed with the President's wishes, observing that he and the President had no secrets. Nonetheless, he did not think Harriman, whose presence would be welcomed at a 'good number of their talks', should be allowed to come between them in their private talks—presumably such as the one in progress. Stalin confessed he did not like Roosevelt's message, as 'it seemed to demand too many rights for the United States leaving too little for the Soviet Union and Great Britain who, after all, had a treaty of common assistance'. Actually, as Stalin must have surely known, the President's message demanded nothing of the kind; if anything, and once the President's electoral sensitivity had been factored out, the message comes closer to John Lukac's image of America's 'supreme unconcern' in the region.

Towards the end of their conversation, the Prime Minister made two final points that were undoubtedly for the Marshal's consumption. First, and in connection with the proposed Allied occupation of Germany, he considered it unlikely that the Americans would stay in Germany, and by extension Europe, for 'very long', the implication being that European problems would have to be settled between themselves. Second, and with no thought of subtlety this time, Churchill personally wanted Stalin to know, to quote from the concluding comments in the record, 'that the British had as many divisions fighting against Germany in Italy and France as the United States and we had nearly as many as the United States fighting against Japan'. Apparently, Churchill was anxious to assure his host that British credentials to speak for the solution of European problems were at least as good as the Americans, who, in any case, were not expected to remain.

What was accomplished?

What precisely, then, did the Prime Minister hope to accomplish by the percentage agreement, such as it was? Unfortunately, and although the documentary record suggests numerous clues, there is no definitive answer to this question. In an official joint communiqué to Roosevelt of their first meeting, Churchill, together with Stalin, merely informed the President: 'We have to consider the best way of reaching an agreed policy about the Balkan countries including Hungary and Turkey,' apparently omitting the concluding phrase, 'having regard to our varying duty towards them', as reported by Harriman. But was there in fact 'an agreed policy'? In an unsent letter to Stalin dated 11 October, the British leader perhaps came nearer the truth when he noted that, 'The percentages which I have put down are no more than a method by which in our thoughts we can see how near we are together, and then decide upon the necessary steps to bring us into full agreement'; and though 'they could not be the basis of any public document, certainly not at the present time, they might however be a good guide for the conduct of our affairs'.

A day later, 12 October, the Prime Minister wrote to colleagues in London further elaborating his thoughts on the percentages. 'The system of percentages', he expanded,

> is not intended to prescribe the number sitting on [the Allied Control] Commissions for the different Balkan countries, but rather to express the interest and sentiment with which the British and Soviet Governments approach the problems of these countries and so that they might reveal their minds to each other in some way that could be comprehended.

More significantly, Churchill added:

> It is not intended to be more than a guide, and of course in no way commits the United States, nor does it set up a rigid system of spheres of interest. It may however help the United States to see how their two principal Allies feel about these regions when the picture is presented as a whole.

To this picture, echoed Eden to the British Under-Secretary of State, Sir Orme Sargent:

> Too much attention should not be paid to percentages which are of symbolic character only and bear no exact relation to number of persons of British and Soviet nationality to be employed [in the Control Commissions].

To the Americans, who were at this stage in the dark, Churchill projected an altogether different, but confident, image of the Balkan talks.

'Everything is most friendly here', the Prime Minister cabled Harry Hopkins on 11 October, 'but the Balkans are in a sad tangle.' In fact, he went on in a manner to justify the continual exclusion of the American Ambassador from the Balkan proceedings thus far: 'We have so many bones to pick about the Balkans at the present time that we would rather carry matters a little further a deux in order to be able to talk more bluntly than at a larger gathering.' On the same day, the Prime Minister indicated to the President that:

> It is absolutely necessary we should try to get a common mind about the Balkans, so that we may prevent civil war breaking out in several countries when probably you and I would be in sympathy with one side and U.J. [Stalin] with the other. I shall keep you informed of all this, and nothing will be settled except preliminary agreements between Britain and Russia, subject to further discussion and melting-down with you. On this basis I am sure you will not mind our trying to have a full meeting of minds with the Russians.

A week later, on the eve of his departure from Moscow, and still in no mood to offer more information than was absolutely necessary, the British leader apprised FDR that 'arrangements made about the Balkans are, I am sure, the best that are possible'. Specifically, the Prime Minister continued:

> Coupled with our successful military action recently we should now be able to save Greece and, I have no doubt, that agreement to pursue a fifty-fifty joint policy in Yugoslavia will be the best solution for our difficulties in view of Tito's behavior and changes in the local situation, resulting from the arrival of Russian and Bulgarian forces under Russian command to help Tito's eastern flank. The Russians are insistent on their ascendancy in Rumania and Bulgaria as the Black Sea countries.

Characteristically, the Soviets had even less to say.

'During the stay of Mr Churchill and Mr Eden in Moscow', Stalin cabled President Roosevelt on 19 October, 'we have exchanged views on a number of questions of mutual interest.' Doubtless aware that both Ambassador Harriman and the Prime Minister had already passed on their estimates of the most important Moscow conversations, the Soviet leader sought to impart his own. 'On my part', he observed with some economy of expression, 'I can say that our conversations were extremely useful in the mutual ascertaining of views on such questions as the attitude towards…policy in regard to the Balkan states', among other things. Furthermore, Stalin stated:

> During the conversations it has been clarified that we can, without great difficulties, adjust our policies on all questions standing before us, and if we are not in a position so far to provide an immediate necessary decision of this or that task…nevertheless, more favorable perspectives are opened. I hope that these Moscow conversations will be of some benefit from the point of view that at the future meeting of the three of us, we shall be able to adopt definite decisions on all urgent questions of our mutual interest.

Stalin's blue pencil tick upon Churchill's half-sheet of paper to the contrary notwithstanding, it is difficult to assess with certitude what, if anything, the Kremlin had hoped to achieve by the percentage agreement.

Perhaps Stalin, not unlike FDR, was more concerned with keeping his Balkan options open than anything else, at least until the dust of the Red Army had settled. There may be more than a little irony in the judgement of one Soviet history of the Second World War, which noted that with the exception of Greece, 'The Red Army's successful offensive in the Southwestern theatre finally buried the plans of the British reactionary circles to forestall the Soviet military presence in the Balkans.' In this sense, Stalin's adherence to the percentage agreement would seem but part of a calculated effort in which to buy time ultimately to bury 'the plans of the British reactionary circles to forestall the Soviet military presence in the Balkans'. And who can deny that the Marshal was an expert at buying time?

Gradually informed of the thrust of the percentage agreement, though, like the principals, by no means certain of its actual meaning, President Roosevelt chose to respond to the critical joint message of his Grand Alliance partners of 10 October in muted tones. 'I am most pleased to know', he replied on 12 October, 'that you are reaching a meeting of your two minds as to international policies in which, because of our present and future common efforts to prevent international wars, we are still interested.' Politician to the core, FDR knew full well it was nearly impossible to find happy solutions for many European problems. This being so, it is hardly surprising that he would want to remain as clear of them as he could, except for those involving Germany. Domestic political considerations aside, it would seem the President revealed his thoughts most clearly when he told Harriman, in a cable dated 11 October, 'My active interest at the present time in the Balkans is that such steps as are practical should be taken to insure against the Balkans getting us into a future international war.' What practical steps Roosevelt had in mind would of necessity have to await the November elections. In the meantime, the State Department responded to the Moscow revival of spheres of influence politics with a programme of its own.

In a memorandum passed on by Under-Secretary of State Edward Stettinius to FDR on 8 November, State declared that:

> [W]hile the Government of the United States is fully aware of the existence of problems between Great Britain and the Soviet Union, this Government should not assume the attitude of supporting either country as against the other. Rather, this Government should assert the independent interest of the United States (which is also believed to be in the general interest) in favor of equitable arrangements designed to attain general peace and security on a basis of good neighborhood, and should not assume the American interest requires it at this time to identify its interests with those of either the Soviet Union or Great Britain.

According to this view, American policy in the Balkans, among other places, should be governed by the following general principles: self-determination, equality of commercial opportunity, freedom of press movement and ideas, freedom for American philanthropic and educational organizations to pursue their activities on a most-favoured-nation basis, general protection of US citizens and their legitimate economic rights, and the proposition that territorial settlements should be left for post-war. However, what impression State's memorandum had on the President's thinking is unknown.

Kennan's realism

On the other side of the State Department spectrum were the views of George Frost Kennan, who at the age of 41 in 1945 was already the senior member of the American diplomatic corps in length of service in Russia. 'I am aware of the realities of this war, and of the fact that we were too weak to win it without Russia's cooperation', the minister-counsellor wrote to his friend Charles Bohlen on the eve of the Yalta Conference. 'I recognize', he continued:

> that Russia's war effort has been masterful and effective and must, to a certain extent, find its reward at the expense of other peoples in eastern and central Europe. But with all of this, I fail to see why we must associate ourselves with this political program, so hostile to the interests of the Atlantic community as a whole, so dangerous to everything which we need to see preserved in Europe. Why could we not make a decent and definite compromise with it—divide Europe frankly into spheres of influence—keep ourselves out of the Russian sphere and keep the Russians out of ours.

For Kennan, such a policy 'would have been the best thing we could do for ourselves and for our friends in Europe, and the most honest approach we could have made to the Russians'. 'Instead of this', exploded the father of containment, 'what have we done?'

Although it was evident that the realities of the after-war were being shaped while the war was in progress we have consistently refused to make clear what our interests and our wishes were, in eastern and central Europe. We have refused to name any limit for Russian expansion and Russian responsibilities, thereby confusing the Russians and causing them constantly to wonder whether they are asking too little or whether it was some kind of a trap. We have refused to face political issues and forced others to face them without us. We have advanced no positive, constructive program for the future of the continent: nothing that could encourage our friends, nothing that could appeal to people on the enemy's side of the line.

Though sympathetic with some of Kennan's arguments, Bohlen was quick to note that the foreign policy he spoke of could not be made in a democracy. 'Only totalitarian states', concluded Roosevelt's interpreter and recently appointed State's liaison with the Executive, 'can make and carry out such policies. Furthermore, I don't for one minute believe that there has been any time in this war when we could seriously have done very differently than we did.' Again, it is not known for certain what kind of impression such ideas had on the President's own thinking.

What is known for certain is that the subject of Balkan percentages was not again raised at the subsequent meeting of the Big Three at Yalta in February 1945, or at any other time. Militarily, the Soviet Union had further strengthened its stranglehold over Eastern and Central Europe. In the place of the October percentage agreement, the broad outlines of which were known to the Americans, the Allies, with Roosevelt at the forefront, now focused on the Declaration on Liberated Europe as the best way of dealing with the future of those countries liberated by the Red Army. Broadly speaking, the Three Powers jointly declared

their mutual agreement to concert during the temporary period of instability the policies of their three governments in assisting the people liberated from the domination of Nazi Germany and the peoples of the former axis satellite states to solve by democratic means their pressing political and economic problems.

Stalin's decision to sponsor unilaterally a minority government in Romania in March, not to mention continuing differences over the composition of the Polish government, suggested both to Roosevelt and the State Department that what the Kremlin really thought about was what Stalin once called 'the algebra of declarations' as opposed to 'practical arithmetic'. Stalin always preferred the latter. To Churchill, it must have appeared as nothing less than the first fruits of 'the pedantic interference of the United States' with his own preferred plans for the division of Europe. Still, the Churchill–Stalin agreements had apparently settled the future of Eastern Europe.

Soviet advances across the heart of Europe during the summer and autumn of 1944 sustained the power revolution that underlay the massive Soviet–German confrontation on the Eastern Front. In September, Kennan wrote from Moscow that 200 million Russians, 'united under the strong and purposeful leadership of Moscow … constitute a single force far greater than any other that will be left on the European continent when this war is over'. That Europe faced the most dramatic power revolution since Napoleon scarcely troubled Washington—and for good reason. The fundamental military decisions demolishing Europe's traditional equilibrium had after all been made in Berlin, not Moscow. It was Hitler's initiation of a two-front war that unloosed the forces now closing in on the Third Reich. It was the savage Nazi assault on the Soviet Union that had motivated the Kremlin's determination to prevent the recurrence of that disaster, a purpose with which few Americans cared to quarrel.

Moscow's ambitions in Eastern Europe and the Balkans expanded in response to the opportunities that flowed from the progress of Soviet arms. After 1941, the Kremlin sought essentially Western recognition of the country's annexations under the Nazi–Soviet Pact of 1939, lands to which Russia had some ethnic or historical claims. In the absence of any restrictive agreements or countervailing power, the Soviet Union, by 1944, was free to act in accordance with its widening interests and ideological preferences. The dynamics of a changing Europe, not some expansionist blueprint, determined what occurred. The necessary Western reliance on the Soviets to deliver it from Germany was carrying a potentially heavy price. Clearly, FDR and Churchill understood that the needed Soviet victories would come with a cost. They never contested the Soviet annexations under the Nazi–Soviet Pact. Nor did Roosevelt ever seriously challenge the personal diplomacy of Churchill and Stalin to divide Eastern Europe into spheres of influence.

Chapter 5

George W. Bush and the Iraq War

Presidential campaigns during 2000 set the stage for renewed conflict with Iraq. Vice President Al Gore, the Democratic nominee, defended President Bill Clinton's record on containment of Iraq, but added: 'I want to go further: I want to give robust support to the groups that are trying to overthrow Saddam Hussein.' George W. Bush, the Republican nominee, went further still, declaring, if as president he found Saddam manufacturing weapons of mass destruction (WMDs), he 'would take him out'. The warning was clear: America's military, as befitting a Great Power, would achieve what diplomacy alone could not. In any case, a red line was drawn, and Saddam was on notice.

George W. Bush was inaugurated the 43rd President of the United States in January 2001, ending the Democrat occupation of the White House. This also meant the appointment of a new selection of secretaries, advisers, and policymakers. National Security Council official Kenneth Pollack, in a final memo briefing the incoming administration on the status of Iraq, with its presumed arsenal of WMDs, warned that containment of Iraq's Saddam Hussein had eroded, and that there were two choices that had to be made—'to adopt an aggressive policy of regime change to try to get rid of Saddam quickly or undertake a major revamping of the sanctions to try and choke off the smuggling and prevent Saddam from reconstituting his military, especially his hidden WMD programs'. Pollack complained that the second option was more difficult because of the lack of consensus in the United Nations Security Council and the unwillingness of other states to match US intentions to confront Iraq.

By the time Bush was elected in 2001, there was a growing consensus in Washington to prioritize a military solution to their diplomatic dilemma with Saddam. Traditional diplomatic engagement—with its carrots and stick approach—had nothing much to show for itself. The solution of military diplomacy, the application of using military might to solve a diplomatic problem, gradually took hold. In fact, it is not an exaggeration to say that American political and military leaders, in their failed efforts to bring Saddam to heel, had come to believe in the inevitability of war with Iraq, first under the rubric of regime change and then in Washington's self-appointed goal of eliminating Saddam's arsenal of WMDs, whether nuclear, biological, or chemical.

Initially, Bush did not seem too preoccupied with the threat posed by Saddam, imagined or otherwise. Prime Minister Tony Blair, in his first meeting with Bush in February 2001, recalled that there was no sense of urgency regarding Iraq. Blair reflected, 'George was set on building a strong right-wing power base in the US, capable of sustaining him through two terms, and was focused especially on education and tax reform.' The only concerns regarding Iraq involved the possibility of reconfiguring sanctions.

Richard Haass, who was now Director of Policy and Planning at the State Department, forwarded a plan to impose 'smart' sanctions on Iraq, based on research he had conducted with Meghan O'Sullivan at the Brookings Institution. The plan was simple. Smart sanctions allowed a larger range of non-military goods to be imported by Iraq, in exchange for an increased revenue stream from Iraqi exports going into accounts controlled by the United Nations instead of Iraq.

The plan was embraced by Secretary of State Colin Powell, and despite scepticism from the rest of the administration, Bush signed off the initiative. Haass noted that the administration understood from the beginning that Iraq was an important foreign policy concern. However, Haass added that what the administration was focused on 'when it came to Iraq was...recasting the sanctions regime. There was a directive to look at existing military plans, but this lacked any real intensity at the time. It was more a dusting off of what was there rather than anything new.' Bush was not inaugurated with a plan to oust Saddam Hussein. In fact, Bush's initial plans to cut government expenditure meant the Pentagon did not receive the funding that was required for a new generation of weaponry, indicating the administration was not projecting any urgency in matters of defence, any advanced plan to confront Iraq included.

The smart sanctions were put to the test at a United Nations Security Council session in June. Despite receiving support from the UK for the revised sanctions—in fact, it was the UK that tabled the draft resolution—there remained significant opposition from the remaining members of the Security Council. Russia was particularly critical of the proposed changes, and Russian Ambassador Sergey Lavrov argued, 'key elements of the United Kingdom draft appear to lead not to easing the very harsh economic situation of Iraq, but rather to tightening the sanctions'. Lavrov explained that by further complicating the list of items that were under sanction, the Security Council was inhibiting, to a greater degree, legitimate trade with Iraq. China agreed with Lavrov's assessment, with Chinese Ambassador Wang Yingfin arguing, 'Foreign companies should be allowed to invest in Iraq, and countries should be allowed to freely sign service contracts with Iraq.' China and Russia agreed that the Security Council was exacerbating and prolonging the humanitarian crisis in Iraq by not relinquishing sanctions.

This time it was the UK's turn to hit back at opposition in the Security Council. British Ambassador Jeremy Greenstock argued, 'it is our responsibility in the Council to prevent Iraq from posing a threat to its region and, as part of this, to ensure that Iraq is fully and verifiably disarmed of its weapons of mass destruction.' Implementing smart sanctions was a step towards streamlining sanctions so that Iraq could not re-arm and lessening the impact of sanctions on the people of Iraq. Greenstock reminded the Security Council, 'we are all aware that Iraq continues to export oil outside the United Nations system to build up illegal revenue with which it can purchase weapons and other proscribed items'.

Although Greenstock was reserved in his arguments against Chinese and Russian opposition, American Ambassador James Cunningham was not. Cunningham stated simply that smart sanctions were designed to prevent Iraq from acquiring the materials it needed to re-arm. At some point in the future the Security Council might revise those limitations, but only 'once there is confidence that they would not be used to rebuild Iraq's weapons of mass destruction or improve its military capabilities'. The USA remained unconvinced that Iraq was disarmed and remained committed to imposing sanctions on Iraq until it was. France, however, found itself between the competing interests of the permanent members. French Ambassador Jean-David Levitte reminded China and Russia that weapon inspectors had been absent from Iraq for two and a half years and their reports were incomplete. However, Levitte argued, 'Recovery requires the return of normal economic conditions.'

The debate was inconclusive, and as a result the introduction of smart sanctions was delayed. That also meant Bush remained confronted by the lingering problem of Iraq. According to Haass, this was not a bad outcome. Reflecting on the proposed policy initiatives to confront Iraq, including forceful regime change, Haass concluded, 'the current and projected situation was not intolerable. Saddam Hussein was a nuisance, not a mortal threat. Trying to oust him, however desirable, did not need to become such a preoccupation that it would come to dominate the administration's foreign policy absent a major new provocation. The United States had more important goals to promote around both the region and the world that would be put in jeopardy were it to get bogged down in Iraq.' The failure of the USA to pressure the United Nations Security Council into embracing revised sanctions only diminished its authority both in the Security Council and over Iraq.

What was unique about the debate over Iraqi sanctions was that it had been opened to non-members of the Security Council, and the majority of the non-Security Council members were overwhelmingly in support of reducing the severity of sanctions and alleviating the humanitarian crisis in Iraq. This support encouraged Iraq's Ambassador al-Qaysi, who complained that Iraq had been antagonized by US airstrikes in early February that destroyed air-defence sites in Iraq. According to al-Qaysi, Iraq was being unfairly and severely punished. Pointing to the voices both within and outside of the Security Council that sided with abandoning sanctions, al-Qaysi explained, 'the faltering of the sanctions regime represents in reality a concrete reflection of the lack of conviction of the majority of the international community'. Smart sanctions that had been proposed by the USA and the UK were accused of being a front for Western companies to receive preferential treatment.

Al-Qaysi asked, 'Do we have any guarantee that those companies are not going to be fat cats of Western origin and be the only ones allowed to buy Iraqi oil?' However, this was beside the point. Al-Qaysi noted that the Amorim report had concluded that Iraq was disarmed and warned the USA and the UK that they could not accuse Iraq of reinstating weapons of mass destruction programmes without evidence. Even UN Secretary General Kofi Annan (Figure 9) had agreed with Iraq on this point, stating in an

9. Kofi Annan—Secretary General of the United Nations.

earlier report on the situation in Iraq that it was imperative to 'put the burden of proof on any side that alleges that Iraq still has weapons of mass destruction'. The result of the open debate within the Security Council was a resounding rejection of the US proposed smart sanctions, and the implemented oil-for-food programme continued without change. Cunningham rued that the Security Council had missed an opportunity to force change in Iraq, declaring that smart sanctions would 'have been adopted today save for the threat of a veto' and despite the objections of non-Security Council members. Although disappointed by the lack of support in the Security Council, Cunningham promised, 'We have made considerable progress and have come too close to agreement to concede the field to Baghdad.' It would take a greater effort from Washington to force change in the Security Council, let alone Iraq.

A 21st-century threat

The terrorist attacks on 11 September 2001 irrevocably changed Bush's diplomatic plans. The death of 3,000 American civilians not only stunned the USA but also reverberated throughout the international community. At the behest of the UK, the Security Council convened a session on 12 September in order to condemn the terrorist attacks where Greenstock explained, 'we all have to understand that this is a global issue, an attack on the whole of modern civilization and an affront to the human spirit. We must all respond globally and show the strength of spirit.'

The attacks had renewed solidarity between the permanent members of the United Nations Security Council, as Lavrov added that the terrorist attacks reminded every nation of 'the timeliness of the task of joining the efforts of the entire international community in combating terror, this plague of the twenty first century'. Levitte, summarizing the collective thoughts of the United Nations Security Council, reminded, 'We stand with the United States in deciding upon any action to combat those who resort to terrorism, those who aid them and those who protect them.' In fact, the offer from the Security Council to confront terrorism abroad supported the new US war footing. Cunningham, proud of the support from the United Nations Security Council, stated, 'we look to all those who stand for peace, justice and security in the world to stand together with the United States to win the war against terrorism. We will make no distinction between the terrorists who committed these acts and those who harbour them. We will bring those responsible to account.'

In the wake of the attacks, the consensus of US intelligence was that al-Qaeda leader Osama bin Laden had organized the terrorist attacks. As one of al-Qaeda's main training facilities was located in Afghanistan, and the Taliban leadership in Afghanistan refused to cooperate with the USA to hand over Osama bin Laden and destroy the training facility, the USA set about achieving those two objectives itself. But, as explained by Philip Zelikow, the administration 'had no plan whatever for ground operations in Afghanistan—none'. The plans against Afghanistan, bearing the blustery codename Infinite Resolve, were little different from when the Clinton White House had looked them over after the October 2000 attack on the USS *Cole*.

Central Command (CENTCOM) commander General Tommy Franks regarded them as 'hardly deserving the title "plan"'. The administration fell back onto a CIA plan to utilize tribal leaders in a loosely based Northern Alliance to agitate the Taliban government, and the USA pushed forward with its objectives to capture Osama bin Laden, destroy al-Qaeda's base in Afghanistan, and expel the Taliban government.

In November, the Taliban government dissolved, and the US military commitment was deemed a success. The lack of multilateral assistance, in a positive reinforcement feedback loop, only confirmed the success of US unilateral action. In fact, Secretary of Defense Donald Rumsfeld had rebuffed an unprecedented offer from NATO for military assistance in combat missions in Afghanistan, determining such a large coalition as tactically prohibitive. By March 2002, the USA began a larger operation against the remaining al-Qaeda members in Afghanistan that led to anti-Taliban tribal leaders consolidating their control across Afghanistan. The war in Afghanistan was considered an overall victory when diplomats from several nations negotiated the formation of a new Afghan government under the leadership of Hamid Karzai, a well-educated tribal leader who was the pick of the Western governments.

Riding a wave of popularity into 2002 as a decisive wartime president, Bush utilized his State of the Union address to lay the groundwork for the next step in what was regarded as a global war on terror. Referring to Iraq, Iran, and North Korea as an 'axis of evil' that threatened the peace and security of the world, Bush made it clear that the next step was to confront those threats. According to Zelikow, National Security Advisor Condoleezza Rice and speechwriter Michael Gerson believed the diplomatic aspect of the State of the Union would focus on the 'nonnegotiable demands of human dignity', in an effort to describe a world 'beyond the war on terror'. However, it was clear that it was Iraq that had returned as the primary concern for the administration and leaked military planning from the Department of Defense in February 2002 confirmed it. In briefings, Bush had 'overwhelmingly emphasized doable operations to defeat Iraqi forces and topple Saddam'. The reconfiguration of strategies to confront Saddam Hussein was inspired by the success of the operations that had toppled Taliban and al-Qaeda forces in Afghanistan. More obvious, the plans focused on Saddam Hussein's intentions as leader and how best to depose him.

By June, Bush's stance on Iraq was clear. In a graduation speech at the US Military Academy at West Point, Bush suggested, 'deterrence could not be relied upon in an age in which rogue states and terrorist groups could acquire weapons of mass destruction', a conclusion that was contrary to the advice of Haass and the State Department. Haass noted that the administration was suffering from diverging advice over plans to confront Saddam Hussein, and 'those who worked with me on the Policy Planning Staff began to come back from meetings around the government and report that those of their counterparts known for advocating going to war with Iraq appeared too cocky for comfort'. With the military success in Afghanistan, the Defense Department had earned a reputation for results, unlike the State Department's efforts to confront Saddam Hussein. As the American media reported that a war was being planned, the administration made sure that there were plans for war, lest they be caught unprepared. By August 2002, Blair remarked, 'at times we would not be sure whether we were driving the agenda or being driven by it'. But Bush waited to clarify the US position at the United Nations in September.

On 12 September 2002, Bush addressed the United Nations General Assembly for the first time. Kofi Annan set the agenda by listing threats to international peace and security one year on from the terrorist attacks in the USA. First, Annan gave priority to the ongoing Israeli–Palestinian conflict. Second, he referred to Iraq's continued defiance of Security Council resolutions and the refusal to readmit inspectors. Annan considered the renewal of weapons inspections as an 'indispensable first step towards assuring the world that all Iraq's weapons of mass destruction have indeed been eliminated'. Third, he stressed the importance of rebuilding Afghanistan in the wake of major military operations. And, fourth, reconciling differences between nuclear-armed India and Pakistan.

Bush's address, however, ignored Annan's list, reinforcing the observation that the USA had already committed to confronting Iraq. Bush stated that the 'greatest fear is that terrorists will find a shortcut to their mad ambitions when an outlaw regime supplies them with the technologies enabling them to kill on a massive scale'. According to Bush, Iraq was an outlaw state that continued 'to shelter and support terrorist organizations that direct violence against Iran, Israel, and Western Governments'. By accusing Iraq of supporting terrorism, Bush had stretched the parameters of the global war on terror to legitimate action against Iraq. In support of the claim that Iraq posed an imminent threat to international peace and security, Bush claimed that intelligence suggested Iraq was in the process of rebuilding its weapons of mass destruction capabilities, a claim that remained unverified because of the lack of international weapons inspectors in Iraq. Bush was convinced that 'Should Iraq acquire fissile material, it would be able to build a nuclear weapon within a year.'

The central purpose of Bush's address was to ignite support for a United Nations sanctioned mission to rectify the situation in Iraq, even suggesting that the United Nations help 'build a Government that represents all Iraqis'. However, there remained no doubt that the appeal to the United Nations for assistance was a take it or leave it proposition. Finishing his address, Bush promised that 'the Security Council resolutions will be enforced, and the just demands of peace and security will be met, or action will be unavoidable, and a regime that has lost its legitimacy will also lose its power'. Indeed, Blair had noticed the shift in the US attitude towards Iraq immediately after 11 September. Blair recalled:

> Saddam had been an unwelcome reminder of battles past, a foe that we had beaten but left in place, to the disgruntlement of many. But he had not been perceived as a threat.

Now it was not so much that the direct threat increased, but he became bound up in the US belief that so shocking had been the 9/11 attack, so serious had been its implications, that the world had to be remade. Countries whose governments were once disliked but tolerated became, overnight, potential enemies, to be confronted, made to change attitude, or made to change government.

Having disregarded Annan's list of prominent threats to international peace and security, Bush was clear that there was a strategic shift in the global war on terror, and that it would focus on Iraq. But, more particular, the strategic shift emphasized Bush's reversal over previous US policy to consider Saddam Hussein's intentions as leader as a higher priority than his capabilities.

On 17 September 2002, the National Security Strategy (NSS) was published, completing the shift to unrestrained US unilateralism. The NSS was clear that the USA was prepared to go to great lengths to confront the 21st-century threat of terrorism. The NSS stressed, 'the United States can no longer solely rely on a reactive posture as we have in the past. The inability to deter a potential attacker, the immediacy of today's threats, and the magnitude of potential harm that could be caused by our adversaries' choice of weapons, do not permit that option. We cannot let our enemies strike first.' This left the USA with the option of 'pre-emptive actions' and 'to forestall or prevent such hostile acts by our adversaries, the United States will, if necessary, act pre-emptively'. The strategy embodied the vision of the world after 11 September that had been encouraged by Condoleezza Rice, a vision that 'the end of the Cold War and the 9/11 attack were bookends for a transitional period in world history'. Zelikow noted that Rice added, 'Before the clay is dry again, America and our friends and our allies must move decisively.'

Even before the publication of the National Security Strategy and Bush's United Nations General Assembly address, it was already understood through diplomatic channels that the USA was moving to war. In July, Sir Richard Dearlove, the head of Britain's Foreign Intelligence Service (MI6), had met with senior US officials in Washington. In a memo from Downing Street on 23 July 2002, Dearlove recorded 'a perceptible shift in attitude. Military action was now seen as inevitable. Bush wanted to remove Saddam, through military action, justified by the conjunction of terrorism and WMD.' And Iraq understood the message clearly enough, pre-empting even the publication of the NSS and readmitting weapons inspectors on 16 September 2002.

The United Nations Security Council spent October negotiating the conditions of the resumed weapons inspections in Iraq. To promote consensus, the Security Council session was an open debate. Kofi Annan set the agenda by admitting, although the readmission of inspectors to Iraq was welcome, 'Iraq has to comply... If Iraq fails to make use of this last chance, and if defiance continues, the Council will have to face its responsibilities.' However, Annan also warned the permanent members of the Security Council, 'if you allow yourselves to be divided, the authority and credibility of the organization will undoubtedly suffer.' It was hoped that by opening the debate over two days, a broader consensus, and cross section of views, might emerge.

A good example was South African Ambassador Dumisani Kumalo, who related the mission to disarm Iraq to the same process of disarming South Africa of nuclear weapons in the late 1990s, warning that the 'pre-emptive' position of the USA might affect the work of the weapons inspections. Kumalo warned, 'it would be tragic if the Council were to prejudge the work of inspectors before they set foot in Iraq'. Kumalo reminded the permanent members, 'The Security Council represents our collective security concerns and should ultimately be accountable to the entire United Nations.'

Contrastingly, Australia's Ambassador John Dauth added his support to the hard-line stance taken by Bush. Dauth agreed with the USA, 'Iraq today poses a clear danger to international security because it has sought to acquire weapons of mass destruction and has a well-established record of using them against its neighbours, and, indeed, against its own people.' Australia remained persuaded that Saddam Hussein maintained his ambitions to acquire weapons of mass destruction and 'in the aftermath of 11 September and, I say with great sadness, the events of 12 October in Bali, the international community must be scrupulous in addressing threats to international security or face the disastrous consequences'. Australia's support had additional strategic value for Bush. Thanks to the ANZUS treaty, already invoked by Prime Minister John Howard for Australia's contribution of troops to Afghanistan, both the UK and now Australia had their interests aligned with the USA and were committed to action.

Hans Blix, United Nations weapons inspector, and Mohamed el-Baradei, Director General of the International Atomic Energy Agency, had also spent October in meetings with US officials in order to detail a proposal for suitable objectives for weapons inspections. Expectations for the inspections varied greatly depending on whom Blix and el-Baradei met in the administration. US Vice President Dick Cheney was upfront and short with the inspectors. Blix reflected that Cheney told them both that he 'in talking about the world at large [always] took the security interests of the United States as his starting point'. However, Cheney warned that the inspections could not continue indefinitely, and that the USA was 'ready to discredit inspections in favour of disarmament'. Cheney's attitude was juxtaposed with that of Bush, who greeted Blix and el-Baradei warmly, and said that the USA had full confidence in the weapons inspectors, promising that the USA would 'throw its support behind us'. These contrasting attitudes were not just restricted to the halls of the White House. In the open Security Council debate, it was the UK that first cast doubt over the weapons inspections process.

British Ambassador Greenstock stressed the importance of an open debate and welcomed the input from non-Security Council members. However, 'The United Kingdom analysis, backed up by reliable intelligence, indicates that Iraq still possesses chemical and biological materials, has continued to produce them, has sought to weaponize them and has active military plans for the deployment of such weapons.' Quoting Prime Minister Tony Blair, Greenstock agreed with the USA, 'the policy of containment isn't any longer working...we know from 11 September that it is sensible to deal with these problems before, not after'.

Ambassador John Negroponte, who had replaced Ambassador John Cunningham, struck a harder line, warning that the United Nations was at risk of becoming irrelevant. Bringing the domestic debate over going to war with Iraq into the United Nations, Negroponte referred to successful legislation just passed through the US Congress that 'expressed support for the Administration's diplomatic efforts in the Security Council to ensure that "Iraq abandons its strategy of delay, evasion and non-compliance" and authorized the use of United States armed forces should diplomatic efforts fail'. Although Blix and el-Baradei had received the impression of some support for the weapons inspection process when they were in Washington, it was now clear from the US stance at the United Nations that that was not the case.

Negroponte added a quote from Bush declaring, 'Either the Iraqi regime will give up its weapons of mass destruction, or, for the sake of peace, the United States will lead a global coalition to disarm that regime.' There was little room for manoeuvre.

Opposing the USA and the UK were the remaining permanent members of the Security Council. Levitte stressed that the 'objective is the disarmament of Iraq. This implies the return of the inspectors and the resumption of monitoring on the ground.' Both the UK and the USA were presumptuous in assuming that Iraq was a threat that required immediate military action, reminding the two states that 'any kind of "automaticity" in the use of force will profoundly divide us'. The Security Council was beginning to understand that the opportunity to restrain the USA had long since passed. For the UK, Blair had decided to back the USA to the hilt. Blair later recalled:

> I was well aware that ultimately the US would take its own decision in its own interests. But I was also aware that in the new world taking shape around us, Britain and Europe were going to face a much more uncertain future without America...So when they had need of us, were we really going to refuse; or, even worse, hope they succeeded but could do it without us? I reflected and felt the weight of an alliance and its history, not oppressively but insistently, a call to duty, a call to act, a call to be at their side, not distant from it, when they felt imperilled.

Blair's 'call to duty' ensured Bush was not alone in confronting Iraq.

Weapons inspections resumed after the unanimous approval of resolution 1441 in November, setting a mandate for UNMOVIC and IAEA weapons inspectors. Although the resolution did not include any approval for the use of force, Negroponte was adamant that should Iraq breach any conditions of the resolution there would be no restraining 'any Member State from acting to defend itself against the threat posed by Iraq or to enforce relevant United Nations resolutions and protect world peace and security'. Greenstock was more measured, reassuring the rest of the Security Council that 'there is no "automaticity" in this resolution. If there is a further Iraqi breach of its disarmament obligations, the matter will return to the Council for discussion as required by paragraph 12.' Such was the attempt by Greenstock to add a layer of moderation to the USA's hard-line stance on inspections.

Although France and Russia voted in favour of the resolution, they reiterated that there was no authority under which any member state could act unilaterally to enforce the resolutions. Chinese Ambassador Wang Guangya confirmed, 'the text no longer includes automaticity for authorizing the use of force'. But it was apparent that the permanent members had greatly different interpretations of the very same resolution. Despite this, Blix noted, 'the differences in interpretation faded into the background in the general delight that the Council had come together and had come out strong'. Although there had been compromise, there was no doubt that the resumption of weapons inspections was an important step in ending the stalemate with Iraq. However, it was a minor victory. There was no doubt that the resolution would not have been accepted by Iraq without the threat of armed intervention by the USA. By 13 November, Iraq accepted all the conditions of resolution 1441.

Inspecting Iraq

On 20 January 2003, the Security Council held a ministerial level meeting to discuss international terrorism. But the meeting, influenced to a great extent by French opposition to a military attack on Iraq, was later described as an ambush. Powell (Figure 10) went into the meeting expecting a discussion concerning terrorism, and instead received a rebuff of US efforts to confront Iraq. Germany's Minister for Foreign Affairs Joschka Fischer explained that he was 'greatly concerned that a military

10. US Secretary of State Colin Powell.

strike against the regime in Baghdad would involve considerable and unpredictable risks for the global fight against terrorism'.

The USA had made clear that it was prepared to go to war with Iraq as part of the global war on terror, and it was only the UK that stood beside the USA's clearly militant posture. Foreign Minister Jack Straw explained the UK support for the USA, adding, 'it is the leaders of rogue States who set the example, brutalize their people, celebrate violence, and—worse than that—through their chemical, biological and nuclear weapons, provide a tempting arsenal for terrorists to use'. According to Straw, there was no doubt that Iraq threatened the international community and, thus, should be confronted in the war on terror.

Despite the unanimity of the Security Council when it had offered to support the USA in a campaign to combat terrorists in

Afghanistan, there was little enthusiasm to repeat the endeavour against Saddam Hussein in Iraq. Russia's Minister for Foreign Affairs Igor Ivanov summed up the general feeling within the Security Council when he warned, 'we must be careful not to take unilateral steps that might threaten the unity of the anti-terrorist coalition'. However, the USA interpreted the mixed response from the ministers at the Security Council as a general underestimation if not misinterpretation of the threat Saddam Hussein posed the international community, something the USA could set straight with its intelligence reports. Powell could only add, 'we cannot shrink from the responsibilities of dealing with a regime that has gone about the development, the acquiring and the stocking of weapons of mass destruction, that has committed terrorist attacks against its neighbors and against its own people and that has trampled the human rights of its own people and its neighbors'. According to Powell, there was no doubt that Iraq presented a threat to international peace and security under the aegis of the global war on terror, and the USA was prepared to confront that threat.

On 27 January, Blix and el-Baradei tabled their first reports of the preliminary UNMOVIC and IAEA weapons inspections. Blix began by clarifying that the Amorim report from 1999 was the foundation for the resumption of weapons inspections. After analysing the report, it was clear that its findings did not 'contend that weapons of mass destruction remain in Iraq, nor do they exclude that possibility. They point to a lack of evidence and to inconsistencies, which raise question marks, and which must be straightened out if weapons dossiers are to be closed and confidence is to arise.' Therefore, the primary objective of UNMOVIC had been to determine the location of documentation that confirmed the unilateral destruction of weapons.

Although Blix admitted that a recent discovery by inspectors of chemical weapon warheads said, by the Iraqis, to have been overlooked in 1991, could 'be the tip of a submerged iceberg',

Iraqi cooperation had been adequate and unobtrusive. However, Blix worried that the Iraqi authorities had not taken the inspections as seriously as they should have, treating the inspectors with a casualness that suggested ignorance towards the situation in the Security Council. Nevertheless, Blix's report produced a balanced appraisal of the situation in Iraq from UNMOVIC's perspective. Blix later reflected that it was not up to him to suggest what the Security Council should do in Iraq, as his task simply was 'to render an accurate report. That was what we were asked to provide and could contribute. It was for the Council to assess the situation and draw conclusions whether there should be continued inspections or war.' Although he privately hoped that the presentation would shock Iraq into cooperation, and out of 'petty bargaining', he did not expect 'the hawks in Washington and elsewhere would be delighted with the rather harsh balance they found in my update'.

El-Baradei, however, was far more precise with the IAEA's recommendations, bolstered by the Amorim report's findings that the Iraqi nuclear weapons programme was fully decommissioned by 1999. El-Baradei stated that after sixty days of inspections 'no prohibited nuclear activities have been identified'. Turning to intelligence that suggested Iraq had attempted to import aluminium tubes machined to standards that were suitable for use in uranium enrichment, el-Baradei explained, 'from our analysis to date, it appears that the aluminium tubes would be consistent with the purpose stated by Iraq and, unless modified, would not be suitable for manufacturing centrifuges'.

More information had to be provided by Security Council members before any other conclusion could be reached. However, where Blix was insistent that he could not tell the Security Council how long inspections would take, el-Baradei was adamant that although inspections would be time-consuming, 'we should be able within the next few months to provide credible assurance that Iraq has no nuclear weapons programme'. Later, el-Baradei reflected that the US response to his report was surprising, especially with regard to the aluminium tubes that had been flagged by US intelligence.

Despite the IAEA reporting that inspectors had found the aluminium tubes to be for use in Iraq's rocket research, Bush went on to state in his State of the Union address on 28 January, only one day after the weapons inspectors gave their reports, that the aluminium tubes were suitable for nuclear weapons production. El-Baradei noted, 'There was no mention of the IAEA's contradictory conclusion based on direct verification of the facts in Iraq. Nor did Bush note the differing analysis of the U.S. Department of Energy.' For all appearances, then, Bush had made it plain that US intelligence was considered more reliable and accurate than weapons inspections.

As the preliminary reports from weapons inspectors did not produce the immediate results that the USA desired, Powell convened a ministerial-level Security Council session in order to present the dossier of intelligence that the USA was using as basis for its claims against Iraq. As was apparent from the presentation, the USA was adamant that Saddam Hussein was involved in terrorism and had concealed his efforts to produce weapons of mass destruction from inspectors. Through intercepted audio from phone calls between Iraqi military officers, reference to satellite images that showed unusual vehicle movement at sites that had been visited by inspectors, and consultation with human intelligence sources, Powell argued that the accusations levelled at Iraq by the USA 'are not assertions, these are facts'.

Further adding to the dossier of US evidence were eyewitness accounts of mobile biological weapons facilities, rendered in illustrations produced by the USA, that confirmed the belief that Iraq was capable of producing anthrax and botulinum toxin. Powell also emphasized the lengths Saddam Hussein had gone to to hide these technologies from inspectors, claiming, 'Call it ingenious or evil genius but the Iraqis deliberately designed their chemical weapons to be inspected. It is infrastructure with a built-in alibi.' Ignoring el-Baradei's report that the aluminium tubes were not part of an Iraqi nuclear weapons programme, Powell, instead, stressed that US experts had certified their use in centrifuge design, and the tubes meant that there was 'no indication that Saddam Hussain [*sic*] has ever abandoned his nuclear weapons programme'. However, it was the link to terrorism that Powell believed would dispel scepticism within the Security Council. According to intelligence sources, Iraq was accused of harbouring al-Qaeda member Abu Masab al-Zarqawi in the north-eastern Kurdish regions of Iraq. Although those regions were outside of Baghdad's control, Powell insisted that Saddam Hussein was involved.

Warning the Security Council that they could not ignore the presence of terrorists in Iraq, Powell explained, 'Ambition and hatred are enough to bring Iraq and Al Qaeda together—enough so that Al Qaeda could learn how to build more sophisticated bombs and learn how to forge documents, and enough so that Al Qaeda could turn to Iraq for help in acquiring expertise on weapons of mass destruction.'

There was no doubt that the USA believed that Iraq had weapons of mass destruction and that Saddam Hussein was determined to use them. It was Saddam Hussein's intentions, as construed by the array of intelligence on Iraq, which seemed to imply his capabilities. Issuing a final warning, Powell stated, 'The United States will not, and cannot, run that risk to the American people. Leaving Saddam Hussain [*sic*] in possession of weapons of mass destruction for a few more months or years is not an option—not in a post 11-September world.' Rice was satisfied that the presentation was the accumulation of intelligence that had been personally vetted by Secretary Powell and had best presented the US case against Iraq. It was, for the USA at least, a 'tour de force'.

Despite Powell's efforts, the consensus throughout the Security Council did not change. For the already persuaded, such as Straw, Powell's presentation was an unnecessary repeat of already established facts, and he chastised the lack of support in the Security Council, arguing, 'the international community owes [Powell] its thanks for laying bare the deceit practised by the regime of Saddam Hussain [*sic*]—and worse, the very great danger which that regime represents'. According to Straw, no matter how powerful the inspectors might be, or how good they were, because of the size of Iraq it was impossible to guarantee that Iraq had no weapons of mass destruction. Resorting to the pre-emptive reasoning of the USA, Straw reminded the Security Council of the international community's past failures at confronting threats, observing, 'at each stage, good men said, "Wait. The evil is not big enough to challenge." Then, before their eyes, the evil became too big to challenge…We owe it to our history, as well as to our future, not to make the same mistake.'

For the unpersuaded, however, Powell's presentation did not offer any solid proof. In fact, it was the opinion of the rest of the Security Council that Powell hand over all his information to the weapons inspectors for verification. Chinese Foreign Minister Tang Jiaxuan was persuaded that the best way forward would be if 'various parties will hand over their information and evidence to [UNMOVIC] and the [IAEA]…through their on-the-spot inspections, that information and evidence can also be evaluated'. Russian Foreign Minister Igor Ivanov sided with China's assessment and appealed to the Security Council to immediately 'hand over to the international inspectors any information that can help them discharge their responsible mandate…they alone can say to what extent Iraq is complying with the demands of the Security Council'.

French Foreign Minister Dominique de Villepin suggested that a third solution to the crisis could be found if the Security Council could agree on a permanent structure for the ongoing surveillance of Iraq. De Villepin explained that a coordinated 'information processing centre...would supply Mr. Blix and Mr ElBaradei, in real time and in a coordinated way, with all the intelligence resources they might need'. Explaining the severity of the dilemma confronting the Security Council, de Villepin added, 'with the choice between military intervention and an inspections regime that is inadequate for lack of cooperation on Iraq's part, we must choose to strengthen decisively the means of inspection'.

Stuck in the shadow cast by the debate among the permanent members was Iraq's Ambassador Mohammed Aldouri, who kept his rebuttal short. Aldouri promised the Security Council, 'if we had a relationship with Al Qaeda and we believed in that relationship, we would not be ashamed to admit it. We have no relationship with Al Qaeda.' And that Powell's presentation was made 'to sell the idea of war and aggression against my country, Iraq, without providing any legal, moral or political justification'. Aldouri's observation that Powell's presentation was more show than substance was later confirmed, by Rice, who explained that the USA was orchestrating a sense of urgency for operational purposes. Rice went on:

> Our sense of urgency was driven by two factors. First, our military forces were approaching levels of mobilization that could not be sustained for very long...it wasn't possible to stand still, since doing so would leave our forces vulnerable in-theater without sufficient logistical support...Second, the President believed that the only way to avoid war was to put maximum and unified pressure on Saddam. That argued for continued mobilization, not pulling back.

Despite the weapons inspections, and despite disagreement within the Security Council, the USA was now prepared to confront Iraq.

On 14 February, the weapons inspectors gave their second report to the Security Council. Blix remained sceptical that UNMOVIC had had enough time to comprehensively understand the situation in Iraq, contrary to Powell's presentation in early February. But there was considerable progress, the inspectors had managed to cover over 400 inspections at more than 300 sites in Iraq, and Blix was adamant that at no point 'have we seen convincing evidence that the Iraqi side knew in advance that the inspectors were coming'. Blix explained that UNMOVIC had an adequate idea of the condition of Iraq's industrial and scientific capacity, and besides the small number of empty chemical munitions that had been found during the initial declaration there had been no further discoveries. However, Blix was hesitant to state that Iraq did not possess weapons of mass destruction, admitting, 'One must not jump to the conclusion that they exist. However, that possibility is also not excluded.'

Although, on one hand, UNMOVIC had made progress in destroying ballistic missile systems that had breached sanctions, on the other hand, inspectors were unable to verify the status of unilaterally destroyed chemical and biological weapons that were outstanding in the Amorim report. Some experts suggested that soil tests might help determine possible destruction sites, but Blix insisted more evidence would be required to assess Iraqi compliance. Blix stressed the good relationship between UNMOVIC and intelligence agencies around the world, and he was satisfied to see an increased amount of information passed on to the inspectors. But, Blix warned, 'we must recognize that there are limitations and misinterpretations can occur'.

Referring directly to intelligence in Powell's presentation, Blix noted that some intelligence had led to sites where there were no weapons, or any activity indicating otherwise. In these cases, intelligence had been useful for 'proving the absence of such items and in some cases the presence of other items—conventional munitions. It showed that conventional arms are being moved around the country and that movements are not necessarily related to weapons of mass destruction.'

Overall, Blix remained unconvinced by Powell's presentation. In his report, Blix had subtly questioned the intelligence that was fundamental to US allegations against Iraq. There was no doubting the importance of Blix's report. Reflecting on the situation as he arrived at the United Nations Security Council chamber, Blix described that he was often mobbed by the media and was often smuggled into the building in a car through a garage. According to Blix, 'it was as if the decision whether there would be a war in Iraq was to be taken in the next hour in the Council, and as if the inspectors' reports on Iraq's cooperation were like a signal of red or green. Although neither was the case, it was a very important meeting.'

El-Baradei, however, was under no such illusion as to the importance of his report as he detailed IAEA progress in Iraq. Since January, the IAEA had been preoccupied with evaluating US intelligence that suggested Iraq had attempted to procure uranium from a source in Niger, and in Iraq the inspectors had uncovered a cache of documents concerning past Iraqi nuclear activities at an Iraqi scientist's house. El-Baradei noted, however, that the documents offered no new insight into previous conclusions that had been stated by the IAEA. The documents had been useful in clarifying aspects of Iraq's previous nuclear weapons programme that were already known to inspectors. El-Baradei's conclusion was concise, stating, 'we have to date found no evidence of ongoing prohibited nuclear or nuclear-related activities in Iraq'.

In the wake of the weapons inspectors' reports, the Security Council once against erupted into disagreement. Blix observed that the debate within the chamber was remarkable because it 'seemed like a pitched battle in which the participants had only seven minutes each to send their words and arguments like colourful tracer bullets through the room'. Once again, a ministerial meeting had been convened to consider the reports.

British Foreign Minister Jack Straw was adamant that UNMOVIC and the IAEA reports were clear that Iraq was in material breach of Security Council resolutions, as there was ample evidence Iraq was not cooperating with inspectors. The only response that would suffice was for the Security Council to 'back a diplomatic process with a credible threat of force and also, if necessary, to be ready to use that threat of force'.

Powell added to Straw's remarks by arguing that no amount of inspections would diminish the threat posed by Iraq, and that 'what we need is immediate, active, unconditional, full cooperation on the part of Iraq. What we need is for Iraq to disarm.' To the USA it was clear that it was unacceptable for the Security Council to wait for inspections to conclude. Powell went on that because of the threat of terrorism, the Security Council could not wait 'for one of these terrible weapons to show up in one of our cities and wonder where it came from after it has been detonated by Al-Qaeda or somebody else. This is the time to go after the source of this kind of weaponry.' This meeting would prove to be Powell's final attempt at securing support in the Security Council, not that Bush believed it was necessary. The final pitch was largely to appease Blair (Figure 11), who was facing his own domestic criticism for supporting the USA unconditionally. As he had promised his own party that he would seek United Nations approval before going to war, Powell was doing Blair a favour by patiently waiting around.

But, the remaining permanent members of the Security Council were unconvinced. Foreign Minister Tang Jiaxuan explained, 'China believes that the inspection process is working and that the inspectors should continue to be given the time they need so as to implement resolution 1441.' Foreign Minister Igor Ivanov agreed, adding, 'we should be guided not by feelings, emotions, sympathies or antipathy with respect to any particular regime. Rather, we should be guided by the actual facts and, on the basis of those facts, should draw our conclusions.'

11. British PM Tony Blair.

However, it was French Foreign Minister Dominique de Villepin who objected outright to the use of force. De Villepin argued, 'The option of war might seem, on the face of it, to be the swifter but let us not forget that, after the war is won, the peace must be built. And let us not delude ourselves: that will be long and difficult, because it will be necessary to preserve Iraq's unity and to restore stability in a lasting way in a country and region harshly affected by the intrusion of force.' There were no guarantees that a military confrontation with Iraq would produce a safer world, nor a more stable Iraq, nor even guarantee that Saddam Hussein would no longer be a threat.

Accusing the USA of acting rashly, de Villepin concluded 'that nothing will be done in the Security Council, at any time, in haste, out of a lack of understanding, out of suspicion or out of fear'. The accusation only added to earlier criticism from de Villepin to Powell at the Secretary General's private luncheon after Powell's presentation in February. It was there that de

Villepin chided Powell, saying, 'You Americans...do not understand Iraq. This is the land of Haroun al-Rashid. You may be able to destroy it in a month, but it will take you a generation to build peace.' The reference to the fifth caliph of the Abbasid dynasty in 786, whose empire extended from the Mediterranean to India, was prescient.

Resorting to war

On 7 March, Blix and el-Baradei gave their final reports to the Security Council, hoping to stress the progress of inspections. The reports would come in the wake of yet another open debate that had been held in the Security Council concerning the situation in Iraq. Blix reported that UNMOVIC had been able to satisfactorily perform inspections without notice across Iraq and was being assisted by increased aerial surveillance, both improvements on UNMOVIC's previous inspection capacity. If the Security Council were to give UNMOVIC enough time, even the outstanding issues regarding additional Iraqi documentation and an interviewing process that was not inhibited by the Iraqi security apparatus could be resolved.

Blix, instead, turned his criticism towards intelligence that had served to underpin allegations that Iraq had reconstituted a weapons of mass destruction programme, noting, 'intelligence authorities have claimed that weapons of mass destruction are moved around Iraq by trucks and, in particular, that there are mobile production units for biological weapons'. Indeed, Powell had been adamant that Iraq was hiding biological and chemical weapons manufacturing equipment in trucks. Blix reported, 'several inspections have taken place at declared and undeclared sites in relation to mobile production facilities. Food-testing mobile laboratories and mobile workshops have been seen, as well as large containers of seed-processing equipment. No evidence of proscribed activities has so far been found.' Blix also responded to intelligence claims that Iraq was storing weapons underground, adding, 'no underground facilities for chemical or biological production or storage have been found so far'.

In order to emphasize the progress UNMOVIC had made, Blix reported that Iraq had taken steps to destroy ballistic missiles that had been deemed in breach of Security Council resolutions. He explained, 'we are not watching the breaking of toothpicks. Lethal weapons are being destroyed.' The remaining tasks for UNMOVIC were difficult to finalize but not impossible, and Blix concluded, 'It would not take years, nor weeks, but months' to conduct the necessary analysis on the remaining unresolved disarmament tasks. Blix maintained that he was in no position to judge whether Iraq was in material breach of Security Council resolutions. However, he had his own definition of his role as weapons inspector. Recalling a conversation with an American colleague, Blix wrote, 'it would have been presumptuous of me to pass such judgment, and he commented "Hans, they wanted you to be presumptuous." Well, yes, if it went their way, but not if it had gone the other way!' Blix's ambiguity did not provide solace for those opposing armed intervention in the Security Council.

For his part, el-Baradei was more direct with the IAEA report. Restating that the IAEA's task was to determine whether Iraq had revived, or attempted to revive, its nuclear weapons programme since inspectors had left, el-Baradei stressed the degradation of Iraq's industrial capacity since the 1980s, when Iraq was known to have a strong industrial base and a fledgling nuclear programme. The overall deterioration of Iraq's industrial capacity was 'of direct relevance to Iraq's capability for resuming a nuclear weapons programme'.

Much like Blix, el-Baradei was critical of some intelligence claims, reporting that the IAEA had conducted tests on the aluminium tubes that the USA had insisted were for use in centrifuges, concluding, 'extensive field investigation and document analysis have failed to uncover any evidence that Iraq intended to use those

81mm tubes for any project other than the reverse-engineering of rockets'. Referring to other claims that Iraq had attempted to import high-strength magnets, el-Baradei explained that IAEA experts concluded that the magnets would be unsuitable for use in centrifuge enrichment facilities. Returning to his earlier report that the IAEA was evaluating claims that Iraq had attempted to import uranium from Niger, he concluded that 'with the concurrence of outside experts...these documents—which formed the basis for the reports of recent uranium transactions between Iraq and the Niger—are, in fact, not authentic'.

Blix remarked later that the USA 'in its uncontrolled eagerness to nail Iraq to a continued nuclear weapons program [would] now have to live with Mohamed's revelation and suffer from its own poor quality control of information'. El-Baradei, however, justified his findings by explaining that 'because many of the IAEA inspectors were returning to well-trodden ground and familiar faces, the Agency was correspondingly more confident in its judgments'. El-Baradei, unlike Blix, was confident that Iraq did not possess nuclear weapons, nor had the capacity to reconstitute its nuclear weapons programme.

Once again, it was ministers who responded to the inspection reports within the Security Council. Powell dismissed the reports outright, claiming, 'If Iraq genuinely wanted to disarm, we would not have to be worrying about setting up means of looking for mobile biological units or any units of the kind—they would be presented to us. We would not need an extensive programme to search for underground facilities that we know exist.' Powell warned the Security Council that the IAEA had been wrong once before about Iraq's nuclear weapon capabilities, therefore, 'we have to be very cautious'.

Referring to the unresolved disarmament issues prepared by UNMOVIC, Powell remarked that the report still indicated Iraq was a threat. Straw was as dismissive of the inspectors as Powell.

The inspections had made no substantial progress since November, and 'It defies experience that continuing inspections with no firm end date...will achieve complete disarmament if...Iraq's full and active cooperation is not forthcoming.' The only option that remained in order to see the disarmament of Iraq, reminded Straw, was 'by backing our diplomacy with the credible use of force'. Straw assured the Security Council that a new resolution, co-sponsored by the USA and offered as a diplomatic pause, asked for a deadline for Iraq to comply with Security Council demands. However, there was no indication that a resolution justifying the use of force against Iraq would be supported within the Security Council. Foreign Minister Ivanov and Foreign Minister Tang openly led the opposition to any resolution that included the use of force to resolve the crisis. According to Russia, weapons inspections were working for the first time in years, and by prematurely ending the inspectors' mission the Security Council lost its authority.

The opposition to Bush's unilateral stance towards Iraq was made more tangible when Ivanov asked, 'What is really in the genuine interest of the world community—continuing the albeit difficult but clearly fruitful results of the inspectors' work or resorting to the use of force, which will inevitably result in enormous loss of life and which is fraught with serious and unpredictable consequences for regional and international stability?' Contributing to the chorus of opposition, de Villepin added that the weapons inspectors had concluded that Iraq represented less of a threat to the international community than it did in 1991, and, therefore, Iraq was effectively disarmed. The obsession with Saddam Hussein's intentions had clouded the USA's strategic vision.

De Villepin addressed Powell directly, and asked, 'Is it a question of regime change? Is it a question of fighting terrorism? Is it a question of reshaping the political landscape of the Middle East?' Although France had sympathy for the USA and its insecurity in the wake of 11 September, on a practical level Iraq had no link to the attacks, and there were no guarantees that the world would be a safer place after a military confrontation with Iraq. Under the circumstances, France was left with no choice. De Villepin stated, 'As a permanent member of the Security Council France will not allow a resolution to be adopted that authorizes the automatic use of force.'

At the conclusion of the meeting, el-Baradei was scathing in his appraisal of the US and UK treatment of the weapons inspectors' reports. Referring to the IAEA, el-Baradei explained that they had spent 'years in Iraq with sweeping "anytime, anywhere" authority. We had crisscrossed the country. We had interviewed every nuclear scientist available. We had destroyed equipment, confiscated records, put the remaining nuclear material under IAEA seal, and blown up the nuclear production facilities at Al Atheer. To liken 2003 to 1991 was an act of deliberate distortion.' In fact, Iraq's ambassador Mohamed Aldouri could only warn the Security Council in his concluding remarks that 'war against Iraq will wreak destruction, but it will not unearth any weapons of mass destruction, for one very simple reason: there are no such weapons, except in the imagination of some'.

Despite US and UK pressure on the weapons inspectors, there was no further support for the US and UK position since the failed attempt in late February to secure a resolution that authorized the use of force. For a second time in only a few weeks, the Security Council held another open debate across two days, showing the widespread opposition of United Nations members to a war with Iraq, other than as a last resort. As the Security Council approached 17 March, the presumed deadline for the beginning of a ground war in Iraq, members in the Security Council attempted to negotiate a resolution that would place conditions on Iraq and suspend the beginning of conflict. The compromise resolution required Iraq to complete a series of tasks that amounted to an ultimatum for the use of force, should any tasks be outstanding.

However, by 14 March, the negotiations were over. An informal Security Council session had heard the concessions, but had produced no consensus, as 'the draft prepared by Chile and five other elected members was withdrawn, the European Union ambassadors met without any convergence, and a meeting of the five permanent members was cancelled. There was no traction except under the tanks in Kuwait.'

In the wake of the failure of the Security Council to support the USA, and in an effort to create a minor coalition despite United Nations opposition, the USA and the UK convened a meeting in Azores, Portugal, for allies that did support the use of force, namely, the USA, the UK, and Spain. It was in Azores, as Rice recalled, 'we sat rather glumly, realizing that a united international community would not materialize. We would take on Saddam either with a coalition of the willing or not at all.'

Not that this bothered Bush (Figure 12) one bit. The statement issued from the meeting was in no way peaceful. Blix noted, as he watched the conference live from New York, that the blame was

12. President George W. Bush.

placed squarely on Saddam Hussein. The leaders 'referred to Saddam's defying UN resolutions for twelve years. The responsibility was his. If conflict were to occur, the U.S. and its allies would seek the affirmation of the territorial integrity of Iraq. Any "military presence" would be temporary.' The statement from Azores would amount to the final declaration of war against Iraq. On Monday the 17th, United Nations weapons inspectors were told to withdraw from Iraq ahead of possible armed action.

This was not the first time, nor would it be the last, that the USA would act forcefully without express United Nations approval. Rice explained, 'From the 1948 Berlin airlift under Truman to the 1999 NATO bombing of Yugoslavia, the coalitions involved were acting without that specific authority.' Rice stated, 'We believed that both Resolution 1441 and the sixteen before it were more than adequate to express the international community's view that Saddam Hussein (Figure 13) was a threat to international peace and security. And, in our view, "serious consequences" had to

13. **Saddam Hussein.**

mean something.' Indeed, even George H. W. Bush had expressed some intention to go to war with Iraq in 1991 without the support of the United Nations. However, in 2003, as the USA split from the United Nations with very few allies, Kofi Annan expressed his disappointment at the disunity of the Security Council. Instead of preventing the humanitarian crisis that had developed in Iraq, 'the conflict that is clearly about to start can make things worse—perhaps much worse'. The United Nations had to ensure there were provisions in place for responding to the post-conflict conditions. However, Annan stressed, 'under international law, the responsibility for protecting civilians in conflict falls on the belligerents. In any area under military occupation, responsibility for the welfare of the population falls on the occupying Power.' Not that the lack of international support mattered for Bush. For Blair, the matter was entirely different. Blair recalled:

> I was about as isolated as it is possible to be in politics. On the one hand, the US were chafing at the bit and essentially I agreed with their basic thrust: Saddam was a threat, he would never cooperate fully with the international community, and the world, not to say Iraq, would be better off with him out of power. My instinct was with them. Our alliance was with them. I had made a commitment after September 11 to be 'shoulder to shoulder'. I was determined to fulfil it.

With UK support, and amidst United Nations warnings, Bush approved the airstrikes that preceded the invasion of Iraq on 19 March 2003. The war with Iraq lasted just over a month, including twenty-one days of major combat operations, in which a combined force of troops from the USA, the UK, Australia, and Poland defeated Saddam. Over 7,000 Iraqi civilians are documented to have been killed, and an additional 17,000 wounded. George W. Bush finally got the war he wanted; the regime change he wanted. And he got his way. The militarization of American diplomacy was complete. A war of choice had inaugurated an era of endless wars.

Chapter 6
Diplomacy in the age of globalization

Diplomacy in the age of globalization has become something
very much more than the diplomacy of states and governments.
It might be urged that it is still true that the legal formalities
based on the Havana Convention of 1928 acknowledge only the
diplomacy of states. Nor can one deny that the entire apparatus
of traditional diplomacy is alive and well. It is relevant, indeed.
This apparatus includes extensive consular networks sustained
by the problems associated with the huge and continuing
movement of peoples which is one of the salient features of our
times, as well as the humanitarian disasters that impact the
daily media.

At another level, states have found themselves forced to alter their
practice of diplomacy, both institutionally and in its external
focus. The most commonly observed results of both of these have
been the reduction of formal representation—for example,
Australia languishes in 20th position of 34 OECD nations in the
number of missions it has abroad (118 total posts), fewer than
South Africa (124), Chile and Portugal (128), and Hungary
(131)—the constant financial crises the diplomatic services
face, the ever-presence of anxious discussions about what state
diplomacy is now actually for, and the consequential emergence
of the doctrines of 'public diplomacy'.

On the ground, though, it is impossible to ignore the diplomacy of the global economic system, ranging from the activities of the TNCs (transnational corporations) to the interventions of the global economic IGOs (intergovernmental organizations), particularly the World Trade Organization (WTO), in the midst of which the world trade order is undergoing a rapid transformation. This transformation challenges those European (small and large) open economies which have been its long-term promoters as members of the WTO and the European Union. However, the WTO-based order found itself in an institutional inertia by the mid-2000s. The minilateral free trade agreements such as the 2016 CETA (Comprehensive Economic and Trade Agreement between Canada, the EU, and its member states) and the proposed TTIP (Transatlantic Trade and Investment Partnership between the EU and the USA) aimed at resolving this inertia. Negotiating them made the EU trade policy one of the main frontrunners in this asymmetric deepening of trade and investment relations. Since the mid-2010s the liberal trade order has, however, been openly questioned by a range of growing protectionist critics. Besides the unilateral threats of import tariffs, real bilateral trade wars, and Brexit contradictions, a long-awaited reform of the WTO, agitated by the US–China trade war, clearly is on the agenda.

All these developments have important diplomatic webs which operate both within and outside the traditional diplomatic system. The same is true of another vast area of diplomatic activity, the diplomacy of civil society organizations (CSOs). In any case, the unfolding saga of phantom, failed, and failing states, civil conflict, and international terrorism has created an entirely new global world of urgent communications between states and NGOs (non-governmental organizations), between NGOs and IGOs, and amongst NGOs themselves.

The defining feature of 21st-century globalization is the increasing complexity of global relations and the rapidity with which information ricochets around the world, opening new avenues for the conduct of diplomacy, while helping new participants to become involved. Globalization, for good or ill, has rendered the world more sensitive to sudden crises such as financial meltdowns and pandemics, however localized they might at first appear. The Great Financial Crisis that arose in 2008, with its cascading effects on to the world economy, was but a cautionary tale. The novel coronavirus pandemic crisis in 2020 (COVID-19), which affected 188 countries and territories, resulting in the loss of hundreds of thousands of souls, millions of confirmed cases, and a battered global economy, was the message writ large. Climate change impacts, which are likely to cause massive issues, are already beginning to have an effect. They will also impact on geopolitics via areas like the Arctic, increasingly ice-free and navigable.

Equally important, the shifting terrain of global relations virtually ensures that security issues of any kind can appear unexpectedly, and rapidly change in shape and scope. Human security risks can usefully be thought of as 'polymorphous', in that, at any one point in time, people and their communities can be subject to political violence, or environmental scarcities, which, individually, can generate a host of future dangers: food and shortages, economic hardship, crime, disease, and human rights abuses. To define a security crisis simply as military, environmental, societal, or financial is to downplay the 'strings' or 'threads' of interconnected happenings, decisions, ideas, and beliefs that shape trajectories of risk.

Complex crises

Human security crises usually 'cluster' around interconnected domains of risk, though there are always problems. In the arbitrary categorization of risks, for example, human security risk analysis tends to falter without an appreciation of the dynamics of interactions between risk factors. Drug trafficking, for example, creates a temporal linkage between the fates of communities in the developed and developing worlds, even if the numbers of individuals involved is quite small.

According to the UN Office of Drug Control (UNODC), over a twelve-month period spanning 2005/6, an estimated 200 million persons used drugs illegally out of a global population of 6.475 billion. Of these, 110 million used drugs on a monthly basis, of whom 25 million, or 0.6 per cent of the global working-age population (15–64), were classed as 'problem drug-users'. The total annual US drug control budget alone stood at US$12.5 billion in 2004, growing to $27.57 billion in 2018—more than three times the value of total US contributions to the United Nations. This is a measure of the scale of the drug 'problem' in America, which extends far beyond the number of addicts, to the corrosive influence of traffickers and the webs of criminal activity that envelop the addicted. Corruption in police ranks and among government officials further corrodes law enforcement and public confidence in government institutions. At the regional level, drug production in Latin America destabilizes legitimate governments and creates de facto 'narco states' in territory beyond central government control.

The grey rhino

Pointing to the metaphorical grey rhino—that highly probable, high impact yet neglected event—former World Bank economist Nicholas Stern early laid out an alarming global scenario on the potential economic and social impacts of climate change. Synthesizing scientific data on climate change, Stern calibrated a sliding scale of natural and human disasters arising from the warming of the earth's atmosphere. A worst-case scenario was predicated on a five-degree Celsius increase in the earth's temperature, causing sea levels to rise, extensive inundation of low-lying coastal areas, and widespread water stress threatening food security in India and China—effectively one-third of the world's population—with obvious consequences for economic and political security at the regional and global levels. Not even the United States could escape the ravages of global warming as the Mississippi Valley region would become a vast inland lake, not to mention all the extreme weather events and wildfires. It took a while for reality to set in, but diplomatic help was on the way.

The Paris Agreement, negotiated by representatives of 195 countries at a UN conference in Paris and adopted by consensus on 12 December 2015, was the first comprehensive global agreement to combat man-made climate change, that is, to deal with greenhouse gas emission, mitigation, and finance starting in 2020. In a perfect world, the idea was to hold the increase in global average temperature to well below 2ºC. The decision of US President Barack Obama (Figure 14) to sign the treaty gave much hope to the climate change movement; President Donald Trump's decision in 2019 formally to withdraw from the Paris Agreement struck a serious blow to the global pact, as the United States was the first country to pull out of the accord. In any case, the absence

14. President Barack Obama at the Paris Climate Accord.

of America as the world's largest economy and second-largest emitter of carbon dioxide proved a serious setback for the climate pact; though Joe Biden's victory over President Trump positions America for a 180-degree turn on climate change, as his administration promises to restore dozens of environmental safeguards Trump abolished and launch the boldest climate change plan of any American president.

Approaching human security

As the Commission on Human Security argues in its 2003 Report, conflict prevention, disease eradication, poverty alleviation, sustainable economic development, food security, and the promotion of human rights are interlinked security concerns. The scope of human security so defined fitted well with objectives outlined in the UN's Millennium Development Goals (MDGs)—eight in total. The MDGs generated new and innovative partnerships, galvanized public opinion, and showed the immense value of the United Nations and its technical agencies setting ambitious goals. By putting people and their immediate needs at the forefront, the MDGs reshaped decision-making in developed and developing countries alike, helping to lift more than one billion souls out of extreme poverty, making inroads against hunger, enabling more girls than ever to attend school, and protecting the environment. There was more.

In September 2015, the UN General Assembly adopted the 2030 agenda for Sustainable Development Goals (SDGs)—seventeen in all, building on the principle of 'leaving no one behind', while emphasizing a holistic approach to achieving sustainable development for all. Strengthening equity, human rights, and non-discrimination, it was a universal call to action to end poverty, protect the planet, and ensure that all people enjoy peace and prosperity by 2030. SDGs benefit from the valuable lessons learned from the MDGs. They also carry forward the unfinished agenda of MDGs for continuity and sustain the momentum generated while addressing the additional challenge of inclusiveness, equity, and urbanization, further strengthening global partnerships by including CSOs and the private sector.

There are major challenges that need to be addressed for achieving the SDGs. To begin with, some of the SDGs that have been costed show that the cost of the SDGs is huge: for example, rough calculations have put the cost of providing a safety net to eradicate poverty at about $66 billion a year. Then, there is the problem of measuring progress—a number of targets are simply not quantifiable; nor have the indicators for measuring such progress yet been identified. Also, there is the lack of chronic accountability for inputs at all levels; this was a problem that was not addressed properly at the MDG level, and there are few signs that this will improve at the SDG levels. More immediate is the maintenance of peace, through diplomacy, broadly defined, in a universe where inequalities run deep, progress is uneven, and the poor remain overwhelmingly concentrated in some parts of the world. Add to this those disadvantaged because of their gender, age, disability, or ethnicity, and an even grimmer picture comes into focus.

The threat to international peace and stability by non-state actors continues to pose a major obstacle for both the Global North and Global South. Frightened and afraid, people are on the move. The United Nations' Global Trends Report—released June 2019—shows that nearly 70.8 million people were displaced at the end of 2018, with 13.6 million newly displaced in that year alone. Overall, 41.3 million were internally displaced persons, most of whom live in countries neighbouring their countries of origin; 26 million were listed as refugees, 57 per cent of whom came from three countries—Syria (6.7 million), Afghanistan (2.7 million), and South Sudan (2.3 million); and 3.5 million were identified as asylum seekers. Put another way, 37,00 people a day were forced to flee their homes because of conflict and persecution. Since the outbreak of the COVID-19 pandemic crisis in 2020, the

United Nations estimates that an additional 247 million souls are marching toward hunger and starvation.

Great Power competition

The end of Moscow-dominated communism, in particular the events of the evening of 8–9 November 1989, when the Berlin Wall came tumbling down, and Christmas Day 1991, when the Soviet Union was formally abolished, foreshadowed the end of the bipolar world of the Cold War, leaving Western policymakers without a conceptual blueprint for navigating global politics. In the place of containment and Mutual Assured Destruction, a gaudy optimism, masked as American 'triumphalism', took hold. Major threats were considered a thing of the past, while the end of history had presumably arrived. Democracy had won the Cold War. Nothing could have been further from reality.

While Ronald Reagan and Mikhail Gorbachev succeeded in halting the Soviet–American nuclear arms race, the subsequent unravelling of the Soviet empire was an unintended side effect of Gorbachev's reforms; termination of the Cold War was not. Though Reagan gets high marks for summit diplomacy, it was General Secretary Gorbachev who broke the ideological straitjacket that had paralysed Moscow and Washington's ability to resolve their differences. Though politically weakened, Gorbachev conceded nothing to US military superiority. Never did he negotiate from a position of weakness. In doing so, he faced greater political, even physical risks. After considering all of this, it is difficult to avoid the conclusion that without Gorbachev, the end of the Cold War could have played out very differently and dangerously.

In the post-Cold War decades that followed, the United States focused its diplomacy on nation building, the war on terror, and humanitarian assistance and disaster relief. The events of these years opened diplomatic avenues that were at once unfamiliar and complex. Into this dangerous and uncertain world, there emerged a new era of Great Power competition. The components of this international system were much more varied, and the line-ups much more difficult to control than in the Cold War.

The new era evoked the recrudescence of the multi-polarity that had marked global politics for at least three centuries before 1939. If anything, it was even more extreme. Most important, the United States pursued an 'America first' diplomatic strategy, harking back to its political isolationism before the Japanese attack on Pearl Harbor. This has opened possibilities for its rivals—Great Powers like the People's Republic of China and Putin-led Russia, lesser ones like Iran and North Korea, and multilateral organizations like the European Union—to exploit American lack of interest by expanding or protecting their own interests. The United Nations seemed to have less and less relevance in maintaining peace and security. Since 2010, but especially since 2017, national interests took primacy over collective concerns, with trading arrangements increasingly negotiated among individual countries. The belief that global economic integration amounted to human progress, which had dominated the thinking of the powers for more than seven decades, was everywhere on the defensive.

And, even if the United States reverted to a more internationalist position after its 2020 presidential election, which is doubtful, the pre-Trump world cannot be rebuilt. Emboldened by America's retreat and their own reluctance to abandon or not expand their gains, China and Russia, with their policy of displacing the USA in the Indo-Pacific and establishing spheres of influence near its borders, respectively, will continue on their course, as well as those of Iran and North Korea, each in search of its own regional hegemony. In this context, regional organizations, with their appeal to multilateralism, will need greater reliance on their own diplomacy.

Diplomacy and multilateralism

Fostering and maintaining an international order based on the diplomacy of multilateral decision-making is not only in the interests of small states and middle powers, which thereby receive a voice in global affairs, but should also be of crucial interest to powerful states, which gain legitimacy for their actions and compliance of smaller states, if they respect and follow rules set up by multilateral institutions. Multilateralism also decreases the costs of actions for all actors by pooling resources—a crucial aspect especially as the world faces environmental, security, and health challenges that will require large investments and inter-state coordination. Nonetheless, the current state of international organizations and multilateral norms has its critics among powerful states, ranging from China and Russia to India and the United States.

Recent years have witnessed individualistic, self-interested actions in international politics that have shaped the current diplomatic landscape. Yet they were more than once met with a multilateral response. The Russian annexation of Crimea in 2014 led to the Enhanced Forward Presence (EFP) and refocusing of NATO on deterrence. Britain similarly contributed to more profound security and defence integration within the EU, as illustrated, for example, by PESCO (Permanent Structured Cooperation by the EU on defence among member states). Can we expect a corresponding response in the case of the collapse of the nuclear arms control regime or Chinese engagement all over the world, through its Belt and Road Initiative or claims in the South China Sea? Equally important, more and more attention probably will be paid to redefining multilateralism itself. Smaller states often have few options besides multilateralism, but new challenges and threats particularly affecting the security of all the major players might require a new diplomatic approach. New challenges, including those posed by the lack of international consensus in the post-COVID-19 world, might well lead to new forms of multilateralism and new bargains among the Great Powers exclusively.

Moreover, Brexit in whatever final form it takes will transform the European Union and its members' diplomacy, while profoundly changing Britain's wider strategic, economic, and political position. Non-state actors will continue to take the initiative in humanitarian development and other fields, once the preserve of governments, by employing 'soft power'—and official statecraft will also rely on this diplomatic strategy. Further add the wicked problems posed by nuclear proliferation, global warming, intense regional warfare, international terrorism, and failed and failing states, and the challenges of 21st-century diplomacy become stark.

Crisis diplomacy

The Center for Preventive Action's annual Preventive Priorities Survey (PPS), in cooperation with the Council of Foreign Affairs, evaluates ongoing and potential conflicts based on the likelihood of their occurring in the near term and their impact on America's global interests, broadly defined. In this way, the PPS aims to help the US diplomatic and policymaking community (and their international counterparts) prioritize competing conflict prevention and crisis mitigation demands. In short, the PPS is designed to advise policymakers where to focus their attention, and at what level, bearing in mind that summit diplomacy seems to be the preferred avenue of choice in the new era of Great Power competition. The problems are not new, easily susceptible to diplomatic solutions, or going away soon. Five stand out above the others.

The first contingency identified in the PPS 2020 survey is an armed confrontation between Iran and the United States or one of its allies over Iran's involvement in regional conflicts and support of militant proxy groups. Tehran's ability to block the flow of oil in the Strait of Hormuz or employ proxy militias in Iraq and Lebanon, among other places, is undoubted. What is unknown is the depth of the resolve of the Iranian leadership to get to that point. The second contingency is a severe crisis on the Korean Peninsula following the collapse of the US–North Korea denuclearization talks and renewed long-range missile testing (Figure 15). On the Korean Peninsula, the primary concern in 2019 was that tensions would increase, following the collapse of these negotiations. The fear since then was that North Korea would continue testing long-range missiles or even nuclear weapons in the absence of negotiations, increasing the likelihood of a crisis.

The third contingency is an armed confrontation over disputed maritime areas in the South China Sea between China and one or more South-East Asian claimants (Brunei, Indonesia, Malaysia, Philippines, Taiwan, and Vietnam). This crisis has been brewing for years, boosted by America's demand to ply these international waters, under Freedom of Navigation. The US–China trade

15. President Donald Trump and Kim Jong-un.

war, with its economic polarization, is an ominous signal that Sino-American relations may freeze into a permanent conflict, and prelude to war. The fourth contingency takes the form of a severe crisis between Russia and Ukraine following increased fighting in eastern Ukraine or a military clash in contested areas. A secondary concern is a deliberate or unintended confrontation between Russia and NATO members, stemming from assertive Russian behaviour in Eastern Europe.

To these should be added a fifth contingency: halting the spread of nuclear weapons. Nuclear proliferation and non-proliferation can be confounding. Given the benefits that nuclear possession supposedly conveys upon a state—more or less securing their independence and protecting them from invasion—the fact that the number of states possessing the bomb is still in single digits (USA, Russia, UK, France, China, India, Pakistan, Israel, and North Korea), far fewer than anyone would have predicted a half-century ago, is surprising. That we don't have definitive answers to the same questions we asked fifty or sixty years ago—Why do states decide to build or not build the bomb? How many nuclear weapons and what strategies are needed to deter? And can the nuclear umbrella be credibly extended to allies?—is equally surprising, if not frustrating. Instead of embracing the intellectual modesty that nuclear statecraft warrants, however, advocates of nuclear abolition and nuclear diplomacy often double down. In any case, nuclear diplomacy can be difficult to practise—whether with Iran, North Korea, or Russia.

In the end, our main preoccupation is understanding why there has not been a thermonuclear war, and what diplomacy can do to continue this streak—a clarion call for diplomacy in action. It is close to impossible to craft a policy about an event that never happened, though there is a strong hunch that nuclear deterrence prevents other states from using their weapons. Deterrence, however, is based on characteristics—fear, resolve, assurance—that are psychological in nature, and hard to observe or measure except after deterrence has failed. The third decade of the 21st century has reached a critical juncture where the nuclear rules of the road, drafted during the Cold War, are gone, and Nuclear Weapons States are rushing to modernize their weapons and delivery systems including hypersonic vehicles. The future of the nuclear regime is in uncharted waters.

British diplomat Jeremy Greenstock reminds us that humans are by nature a contentious and destructive species, and so every opportunity for peaceful interaction ought to be maximized. This is his polite way of saying that diplomacy and war remain two sides of the same coin, and that without the greatest attention to the former, one could—and should—expect violence to resolve the great issues of the day. Historically, this has always been so, and not much has changed in this respect from the time that Thucydides wrote about the Peloponnesian War in the 5th century BC. What have changed of course are the weapons and magnitude of the level of violence at the disposal of our contrary species. In this sense, diplomacy remains the first and last line of defence against disaster and is thus worthy of serious attention. It is why the study of diplomacy through history matters.

References and further reading

Preface

David Reynolds's observation on the origins of diplomacy is in
   Summits: Six Meetings That Shaped the Twentieth Century (Basic
   Books, 2007). The Nicolson, Catlin, Toynbee, and Kissinger quotes
   are found, respectively, in: K. J. Holsti, *Taming the Sovereigns:
   Institutional Change in International Politics* (Cambridge
   University Press, 2004); Joseph M. Siracusa, *Diplomacy: A Very
   Short Introduction* (Oxford University Press, 2010);
   Daniel M. Smith and Joseph M. Siracusa, *The Testing of America,
   1914–1945* (Forum Press, 1979); and Henry Kissinger, *Diplomacy*
   (Simon and Schuster, 1994).

Chapter 1: Evolution of diplomacy

To begin at the beginning, see Harold Nicolson's classic study of the
   history of diplomacy, *Diplomacy* (Harcourt Brace, 1939), which is
   not to be confused with Henry Kissinger's otherwise brilliant study
   of diplomatic history, *Diplomacy* (Simon and Schuster, 1994),
   which, Kissinger assures us, is quite different in scope, intentions,
   and ideas. Indispensable is M. S. Anderson's treatise on the
   evolution of diplomacy to 1919, *The Rise of Modern Diplomacy,
   1450–1919* (Longman, 1993). The history of diplomacy is admir-
   ably covered in G. R. Berridge, *Diplomacy: Theory and Practice*,
   5th edn (Palgrave Macmillan, 2015); Keith Hamilton and Richard
   Langhorne, *The Practice of Diplomacy: Its Evolution, Theory and
   Administration*, 2nd edn (Routledge, 2010); and Adam Watson,
   Diplomacy: Dialogue between States (Routledge, 1982). For a

critique of the culture of traditional diplomatic services, see Shaun
Riordan, *The New Diplomacy* (Polity Press, 2002).

How diplomats represent state institutions in a complex relationship
of facts designed to bring order to international society is explored
in Paul Sharp and Geoffrey Wiseman (eds), *The Diplomatic Corps
as an Institution of International Society* (Palgrave Macmillan,
2008). G. R. Berridge, a leading authority on the history of
diplomacy, has much to say in *Return to the United Nations: UN
Diplomacy in Regional Conflicts* (Palgrave Macmillan, 1991). For
the emerging diplomacy of civil society, see Paul Battersby and
Joseph M. Siracusa, *Globalization and Human Security* (Rowman
and Littlefield, 2009). Quotes on public diplomacy are taken from
Charles Wolf, Jr, and Brian Rosen, *Public Diplomacy: How To
Think About It and Improve It* (RAND, 2004). Also useful is
Holsti, *Taming the Sovereigns*.

For the history and significance of treaties, see Mario Toscano, *The
History of Treaties and International Politics* (Johns Hopkins
University Press, 1966); Eileen Denza, *Diplomatic Law*, 3rd edn
(Oxford University Press, 2008); and Joseph M. Siracusa,
'Treaties', in Nigel Young (ed.), *The Oxford International
Encyclopedia of Peace*, 4 vols (Oxford University Press, 2010).

Chapter 2: Diplomacy of the American Revolution

The best summary of the diplomacy of the American Revolution is
Samuel Flagg Bemis, *The Diplomacy of the American Revolution*
(D. Appleton-Century, 1935). Bemis skilfully exploits archives in
offering a Whig interpretation of an innocent America dealing with
corrupt Europe. This interpretation has been challenged, but not
the coverage and detailed analysis. In support of Bemis, see
Norman A. Graebner, Richard Dean Burns, and Joseph M. Siracusa,
*Foreign Affairs and the Founding Fathers, from the Confederation to
Constitution, 1776–1787* (Praeger, 2011). Also useful are
Jonathan R. Dull, *A Diplomatic History of the American Revolution*
(Yale University Press, 1985); and Reginald Horsman, *The
Diplomacy of the New Republic* (Harlan Davidson, 1985).

Arthur M. Schlesinger's *The Colonial Merchants and the American
Revolution, 1763–1776* (Longmans, 1918) is a landmark study of
the origins of the American Revolution, showing the role merchants
played in staving off radical measures of Parliament and colonials
until 1776.

The best general account of British ministerial politics and the American question for 1773 to 1775 is Bernard Donoghue, *British Politics and the American Revolution, the Path to War, 1773–75* (Macmillan, 1964). For a description of British military objectives and successes, see Piers Mackesy, *The War for America, 1775–1783* (University of Nebraska Press, 1993). William C. Stinchcombe, *The American Revolution and the French Alliance* (Syracuse University Press, 1969) analyses the domestic reaction to the French alliance in America, making the case that colonial Americans suspended their traditional anti-French and anti-Catholic beliefs to make it a success. For a discussion of domestic and international factors and influences, consult Richard W. Van Alstyne, *Empire and Independence: The International History of the American Revolution* (John Wiley, 1965).

Benjamin Franklin was the most important diplomat of the American Revolution and because of this has attracted much scholarly attention. The best studies of Franklin and his times are Claude A. Lopez and Eugenia W. Herbert, *The Private Franklin: The Man and his Family* (Norton, 1975); Gerald Stourzh, *Benjamin Franklin and American Foreign Policy* (University of Chicago Press, 1954); and Carl Van Doren, *Benjamin Franklin* (Viking, 1938).

The standard account of Henry Laurens, John Adams, Benjamin Franklin, and particularly John Jay, who negotiated the peace with Great Britain in 1782, is Richard B. Morris, *The Peacemakers: The Great Powers and American Independence* (Harper and Row, 1965). Valuable insights are found in Lawrence S. Kaplan, 'The Treaty of Paris 1783: A Historiographical Challenge', *International History Review*, 5 (August 1983), 431–42; and Ronald Hoffman and Peter J. Albert (eds), *Peace and Peacemakers: The Treaty of 1783* (University of Virginia Press for the United States Capitol Historical Society, 1986). The Royal Instructions to the Peace Commission of 1778 are conveniently located in S. E. Morison (ed.), *Sources and Documents Illustrating the American Revolution, 1764–1788* (The Clarendon Press, 1923).

Chapter 3: Diplomatic origins of the Great War and Versailles

The best general introductions to European history covered by this chapter are Norman Rich, *Great Power Diplomacy, 1814–1914* (McGraw-Hill, 1992); A. J. P. Taylor, *The Struggle for Mastery*

in Europe, 1848–1918 (Oxford University Press, 1954);
Christopher J. Bartlett, *The Global Conflict: The International Rivalry of the Great Powers, 1880–1990* (Longman, 1994);
Norman Stone, *Europe Transformed, 1878–1919* (Oxford University Press, 1999); and James Joll, *Europe since 1870*, 4th edn (Penguin, 1990). Nineteenth-century diplomacy is treated in Christopher J. Bartlett, *Peace, War and the European Powers, 1814–1914* (Palgrave Macmillan, 1996); and F. R. Bridge and Roger Bullen, *The Great Powers and the European States System, 1815–1914* (Longman, 1980). Useful access to primary source material is provided by Ralph R. Menning (ed.), *The Art of the Possible: Documents on Great Power Diplomacy, 1814–1914* (McGraw-Hill, 1996).

For the breakdown of Bismarck's alliance system, see Richard Langhorne, *The Collapse of the Concert of Europe: International Politics, 1890–1914* (Palgrave Macmillan, 1981); William L. Langer, *The Franco-Russian Alliance, 1890–1894* (Harvard University Press, 1929) and *The Diplomacy of Imperialism*, 2nd edn (Knopf, 1968); and George F. Kennan, *The Decline of Bismarck's European Order: Franco-Russian Relations, 1875–1890* (Princeton University Press, 1979).

James Joll and Gordon Martel, *The Origins of the First World War*, 3rd edn (Oxford University Press, 2006) and Christopher Clark's *The Sleepwalkers: How Europe Went to War in 1914* (Penguin, 2013) are easily the two best books ever written on the subject, while the best military history of the First World War is B. H. Liddell Hart, *History of the First World War* (Weidenfeld and Nicolson, 1970). For the harm done on the ground level, see Alan Kramer, *Dynamic of Destruction: Culture and Mass Killing in the First World War* (Oxford University Press, 2007); and Alexander Watson, *Enduring the Great War: Combat, Morale and Collapse in the German and British Armies, 1914–1918* (Cambridge University Press, 2008).

For the entry of the United States into the war and its subsequent rejection of the Treaty of Versailles, see Thomas J. Knock, *To End All Wars: Woodrow Wilson and the Quest for a New World Order* (Princeton University Press, 1995); Daniel M. Smith, *The Great Departure: United States and World War I, 1914–1920* (Wiley, 1965); and Arthur S. Link, *Wilson, the Diplomatist* (Johns Hopkins University Press, 1957).

For Germany's 'September Programme', see Fritz Fischer, *Germany's War Aims in the First World War* (Norton, 1967). Fischer lays the blame for war squarely on Berlin. Jay Winter and Antoine Prost's *The Great War in History: Debates and Controversies, 1914 to the Present* (Cambridge University Press, 2006) is an important comparative study, analysing a multitude of books on the First World War written by French, British, and German scholars in order to show patterns of themes and methods over time.

For the historical debate surrounding the course and consequences of the Treaty of Versailles, see Manfred F. Boemeke, Gerald D. Feldman, and Elisabeth Glaser (eds), *The Treaty of Versailles: A Reassessment after 75 Years* (Cambridge University Press, 1998). Quotes by David Lloyd George, Winston Churchill, and John Maynard Keynes in this chapter are found in David Lloyd George, *British War Aims* (George H. Doran, 1917) and *War Memoirs* (Little Brown, 1932–7); Winston Churchill, *The World Crisis* (Butterworth, 1923–31), vol. 5; and John Maynard Keynes, *The Economic Consequences of the Peace* (Harcourt, Brace and Howe, 1920), respectively.

Chapter 4: The night Stalin and Churchill divided Europe

Before all else, I should like to pay tribute to John Lukacs, whose 'The Night Stalin and Churchill Divided Europe', *The New York Times Magazine*, 5 October 1969, 37–50, inspired a generation of scholarship, including my own. See Joseph M. Siracusa, *Into the Dark House: American Diplomacy and the Ideological Origins of the Cold War* (Regina Books, 1998); 'The Night Stalin and Churchill Divided Europe: The View from Washington', *Review of Politics* 3 (Fall 1981), 381–409; and 'The Meaning of TOLSTOY: Churchill, Stalin, and the Balkans, Moscow, October 1944', *Diplomatic History*, 3 (Fall 1979), 443–63, which is a discussion of the source material for this meeting located in the Public Record Office. Also useful are Albert Resis, 'The Churchill–Stalin Secret "Percentages" Agreement on the Balkans, Moscow, October 1944', *American Historical Review*, 85 (1981), 368–87, and 'Spheres of Influence in Soviet Diplomacy', *Journal of Modern History*, 53 (1981), 417–39; and Vojtech Mastny, *Russia's Road to the Cold War: Diplomacy, Warfare, and the Politics of Communism, 1941–1945* (Columbia University Press, 1979).

Recommended overviews of the war years include the first volume in Norman A. Graebner, Richard Dean Burns, and Joseph M. Siracusa, *America and the Cold War, 1941–1991: A Realist Interpretation*, 2 vols (Praeger Security International, 2010); Gerhard L. Weinberg, *A World at Arms: A Global History of World War II* (Cambridge University Press, 1994); and Herbert Feis, *Churchill, Roosevelt, Stalin: The War They Waged and the Peace They Sought* (Princeton University Press, 1957). On the British side, see Sir Llewellyn Woodard, *History of the Second World War: British Foreign Policy in the Second World* War, 5 vols (HMSO, 1970–6) and John Charmley, *Churchill's Grand Alliance: The Anglo-American Special Relationship, 1940–57* (Hodder and Stoughton, 1995). The indispensable reference work for the period is *The Oxford Companion to the Second World War*, ed. I. C. B. Dear (Oxford University Press, 1995).

Winston Churchill's recollection of events is found in chapter 15, 'October in Moscow', in *The Second World War*, vol. 6, *Triumph and Tragedy* (Houghton Mifflin, 1953). Also useful are *The Diaries of Sir Alexander Cadogan, 1939–45*, ed. David Dilks (Cassell, 1971); Anthony Eden, *The Memoirs of Anthony Eden, Earl of Avon: The Reckoning* (Houghton Mifflin, 1965); W. Averell Harriman and Elie Abel, *Special Envoy to Churchill and Stalin, 1941–1946* (Random House, 1975); R. E. Sherwood, *Roosevelt and Hopkins: An Intimate History* (Putnam's, 1977); Charles E. Bohlen, *Witness to History, 1929–1969* (Norton, 1973); and George F. Kennan, *Memoirs, 1925–1963* (Little, Brown, 1967).

Chapter 5: George W. Bush and the Iraq War

The best place to begin is Kenneth M. Pollack, *The Threatening Storm: The Case for Invading Iraq* (Random House, 2002); Richard N. Haass, *War of Necessity, War of Choice: A Memoir of Two Iraq Wars* (Simon & Schuster, 2009); and James Mann, *Rise of the Vulcans: The History of Bush's War Cabinet* (Viking, 2004). The United Nations side of the Second Gulf War is told in Hans Blix, *Disarming Iraq: The Search for Weapons of Mass Destruction* (Bloomsbury, 2005); Mohamed El-Baradei, *The Age of Deception: Nuclear Diplomacy in Treacherous Times* (Bloomsbury, 2011); and Alexander Thompson, *Channels of Power: The UN Security Council and U.S. Statecraft* (Cornell University Press, 2009). Philip Zelikow's views and US public opinion are located, respectively, in

Philip Zelikow, 'US Strategic Planning in 2001–2002', in Melvyn Leffler and Jeffrey W. Legro (eds), *In Uncertain Times: American Foreign Policy after the Berlin Wall and 9/11* (Cornell University Press, 2011) and Oli R. Holsti, *American Public Opinion on the Iraq War* (University of Michigan Press, 2011). For quotes from the British Prime Minister, see Tony Blair, *A Journey* (Knopf, 2010); and for George W. Bush's National Security Adviser, Condoleezza Rice, *No Higher Honor: A Memoir of my Years in Washington* (Random House, 2011). Quotes from Vice President Al Gore and Presidential candidate George W. Bush are found in Richard Dean Burns, Joseph M. Siracusa, and Jason Flanagan, *American Foreign Relations since Independence* (Praeger, 2013).

Chapter 6: Diplomacy in the age of globalization

An ideal place to begin is Manfred Steger's *Globalization: A Very Short Introduction* (4th edn, Oxford University Press, 2017). Also useful is Manfred Steger, Paul Battersby, and Joseph M. Siracusa (eds), *The SAGE Handbook of Globalization*, 2 vols (SAGE, 2014).

A starting point for the concept of human security is Battersby and Siracusa, *Globalization and Human Security*. For critical perspectives, see Giorgio Shani, Makoto Sato, and Mustapha Kamal Pasha (eds), *Protecting Human Security in a Post 9/11 World: Critical and Global Insights* (Palgrave Macmillan, 2007). Also useful are International Commission on Intervention and State Sovereignty, *The Responsibility to Protect* (International Development Research Center, 2001) and Andrew Mack, *The Human Security Report 2005: War and Peace in the 21st Century* (Oxford University Press, 2005).

An assessment of the end of the Cold War and the events that followed is found in Norman A. Graebner, Richard Dean Burns, and Joseph M. Siracusa, *Reagan, Bush, Gorbachev: Revisiting the End of the Cold War* (Praeger, 2008); Leffler and Legro (eds), *In Uncertain Times*; and Timothy Lynch, *In the Shadow of the Cold War: American Foreign Policy from George Bush Sr. to Donald Trump* (Cambridge University Press, 2019). The best introduction to the recrudescence of Great Power competition is Matthew Kroenig, *The Return of Great Power Rivalry: Democracy Versus Autocracy from the Ancient World to the U.S. and China* (Oxford University Press, 2020).

The Stern and Greenstock quotes are found, respectively, in Nicholas
Stern, *The Stern Review: The Economics of Climate Change* (HM
Treasury, 2006) and Richard Dean Burns and Joseph M. Siracusa,
International Diplomacy and the Pursuit of Global Security
(Regina Books, 2010).

Index

For the benefit of digital users, indexed terms that span two pages (e.g., 52–53) may, on occasion, appear on only one of those pages.

DIPLOMACY
A Very Short Introduction
Joseph M. Siracusa

Like making war, diplomacy has been around a very long time, at least since the Bronze Age. It was primitive by today's standards, there were few rules, but it was a recognizable form of diplomacy. Since then, diplomacy has evolved greatly, coming to mean different things, to different persons, at different times, ranging from the elegant to the inelegant. Whatever one's definition, few could doubt that the course and consequences of the major events of modern international diplomacy have shaped and changed the global world in which we live. Joseph M. Siracusa introduces the subject of diplomacy from a historical perspective, providing examples from significant historical phases and episodes to illustrate the art of diplomacy in action.

'Professor Siracusa provides a lively introduction to diplomacy through the perspective of history.'

Gerry Woodard, Senior Fellow in Political Science at the University of Melbourne and former Australasian Ambassador in Asia

www.oup.com/vsi

GEOPOLITICS
A Very Short Introduction
Klaus Dodds

In certain places such as Iraq or Lebanon, moving a few feet either side of a territorial boundary can be a matter of life or death, dramatically highlighting the connections between place and politics. For a country's location and size as well as its sovereignty and resources all affect how the people that live there understand and interact with the wider world. Using wide-ranging examples, from historical maps to James Bond films and the rhetoric of political leaders like Churchill and George W. Bush, this Very Short Introduction shows why, for a full understanding of contemporary global politics, it is not just smart - it is essential - to be geopolitical.

'Engrossing study of a complex topic.'

Mick Herron, Geographical.

INTERNATIONAL RELATIONS
A Very Short Introduction
Paul Wilkinson

Of undoubtable relevance today, in a post-9-11 world of growing political tension and unease, this *Very Short Introduction* covers the topics essential to an understanding of modern international relations. Paul Wilkinson explains the theories and the practice that underlies the subject, and investigates issues ranging from foreign policy, arms control, and terrorism, to the environment and world poverty. He examines the role of organizations such as the United Nations and the European Union, as well as the influence of ethnic and religious movements and terrorist groups which also play a role in shaping the way states and governments interact. This up-to-date book is required reading for those seeking a new perspective to help untangle and decipher international events.

www.oup.com/vsi

LEADERSHIP
A Very Short Introduction
Keith Grint

In this *Very Short Introduction* Keith Grint prompts the reader to rethink their understanding of what leadership is. He examines the way leadership has evolved from its earliest manifestations in ancient societies, highlighting the beginnings of leadership writings through Plato, Sun Tzu, Machiavelli and others, to consider the role of the social, economic, and political context undermining particular modes of leadership. Exploring the idea that leaders cannot exist without followers, and recognising that we all have diverse experiences and assumptions of leadership, Grint looks at the practice of management, its history, future, and influence on all aspects of society.

www.oup.com/vsi

THE UNITED NATIONS

A Very Short Introduction

Jussi M. Hanhimäki

With this much-needed introduction to the UN, Jussi Hanhimäki engages the current debate over the organization's effectiveness as he provides a clear understanding of how it was originally conceived, how it has come to its present form, and how it must confront new challenges in a rapidly changing world. After a brief history of the United Nations and its predecessor, the League of Nations, the author examines the UN's successes and failures as a guardian of international peace and security, as a promoter of human rights, as a protector of international law, and as an engineer of socio-economic development.

www.oup.com/vsi